THE STYLE
OF AN
ENGLISHMAN

THE STYLE

OF AN

ENGLISHMAN

AND HOW TO ACHIEVE IT

NICKY SMITH

FOREWORD BY NIGEL HAVERS

MICHAEL JOSEPH · LONDON

ALFRED DUNHILL

FASHION AND ACCESSORIES FOR MEN

To Edmund de Rothschild for his invaluable assistance

and to S.A.W., also a man of style.

MICHAEL JOSEPH LTD

Published by the Penguin Group
27 Wrights Lane London W8 5TZ. England

Viking Penguin Inc.
40 West 23rd Street, New York, New York 10010, USA
Penguin Books Australia Ltd
Ringwood, Victoria, Australia
Penguin Books Canada Ltd
2801 John Street, Markham, Ontairo, Canada L3R 1B4
Penguin Books (NZ) Ltd.
182–190 Wairau Road, Auckland 10, New Zealand

Penguin Books Ltd. Registered Office
Harmondsworth, Middlesex, England.

First published in Great Britain in 1989

Illustrations © Alfred Dunhill Ltd, except those listed below
© Michael Joseph Ltd
Chris Grout Smith 14, 15, 21, 22, 23, 32, 35, 38, 39, 42, 45, 49,
81, 87, 88, 89, 111, 152, 163, 173
Peter Wood 113, 144, 145, 149
Mike Rocket 37, 54, 56, 115, 126, 129, 132
The following photographs were reproduced by kind permission
of the copyright holders:
Tim Graham 93, 121
Rex Features Ltd. 161
British Wool 41

Design and Art Direction
Graham Davis Associates

Typeset by Goodfellow and Egan, Cambridge
Colour reproduction by Scantrans, Singapore
Printed and bound by Kyodo-Shing Loong Printing,
Singapore

A CIP catalogue record for this book is available
from the British Library

ISBN 0 7181 3163 0

CONTENTS

AUTHOR'S ACKNOWLEDGEMENTS:

It is impossible to acknowledge all those who offered help and advice for this book, especially the young men about town, at sea, at parties, in pubs and wine bars, at corporate cocktails and on the playing fields of England who provided ready and often unintended inspiration. But there are a few to whom I am particularly indebted.

First, my thanks go to the contributors of quotes. All those who did, quoted with style, good humour and a great deal of tolerance but Lord Lichfield must surely be given the accolade of 'most stylish' for ringing me back on a day which he had already spent photographing, flying home from New York and starting a restaurant. Some who declined, also did so with style, especially Michael Heseltine, Kingsley Amis ("off the cuff, I am afraid I have no thoughts on dress or behaviour"), Ned Sherrin, who sent me a copy of a fan letter advising him to 'get a new outfit' at once, Ed Victor, Sir Adrian Swire, Lord Linley, Terry Wogan and Robin Janvrin, Press Secretary to The Queen who wrote on behalf of the male royals while he was 'at sea' in Australia. Denis Thatcher's reply, written in ink on the back of my own carefully typed letter, was so 'stylish' it is reproduced in full in chapter five.

Second, I would like to thank the many retailers who gave advice or lent photographic props, including, in some sort of alphabetic order, Alfred Dunhill Ltd., Anthony Price, Asprey, Aquascutum, Austin Read, Blazer, Crolla, Fox Brothers of Tunbridge Wells, Hackett, Hamnett, Lock and Sons, Malcolm Levene, Moss Bros, Next, Simpson's of Piccadilly, Paul Smith, Powell and Co, Stephen King, Sun and Snow, Tommy Nutter, Thomas Pink, Woodhouse and Captain O.M. Watts.

Special help however came from Sir Monty Moss, Mr Nicholls at Etheridge and Glasspool Ltd, Mr Justice at Couch and Hoskins, Robert Jenkins and Jan Stoneham at Selfridges, Mr Glasgow and Mr O Flynn at New and Lingwood, David Cooper of Glemby International, Sir Thomas Lethbridge of Swayne, Adeney Brigg, Mr Richards of Holland and Holland, Peter Tilley, Maurice Gregg and Sarah Clarke of Alfred Dunhill Limited, Chrissie Probert and Philippa Gimlet, formerly of Men in Vogue, Hamish Bowles of Harpers and Queen, Julia Bayley of the Royal Yachting Association, Anne Birrell of Nigel French, Trevor Mound and Ivor Roberts of the Foreign and Commonwealth Office whose comments on 'uniform', official style and protocol were invaluable, Beth Barrington Haines for advice on Polo, Amanda Hemingway and Victor Olliver of Woman's Journal for technical encouragement and Peter York for his invaluable advice and generous supply of copies of his books.

Third, a book like this is never the work of one person but the combined anguish of a team and this book would not have happened without designers Graham Davis and Kevin Ryan, contributing photographers Chris Grout-Smith and Peter Wood, stylist Erika Pek and models Les Robertson and PC Anderson. Most of all it needed the inspired energy of Vivien James, the quiet good sense of Peter Robinson, the constant optimism of Suzee Kornfeld and, most of all, the generous support of Libby Danson.

Final thanks must go to Roger Schlesinger for his professional support, his stylish example and his genuine kindness, to Russell Twisk, Editor-in-Chief of the Reader's Digest, for his patience during the final stages of the work and to JDF Jones, Arts Editor of the Financial Times who first had the courage to publish the unmentionable and thereby gave me the basis for this book.

FOREWORD

The introduction of THE STYLE OF AN ENGLISHMAN talks of the concept of the English gentleman, the ageless and quintessentially British character whose appeal is international and whose style, modelled on the confirmed wisdom of tradition, 'is the envy of everyone'. There, encapsulated in a few words, is the real theme of this excellent and thoroughly enjoyable book. Instead of just promoting some new trend or fad in sartorial elegance, this book shows you not only the 'how' but also the 'why'. Here is a clear, concise account of the Englishman's 'style', with exhaustive and invaluable practical advice on everything from the optimum execution of the morning shave, to achieve a mirror-like sheen on your shoes.

There can be little doubt that the Englishman's style, once the preserve of very few, now affects us all in one way or another. Fashions may change, but that intangible, very distinctive quality, which one might almost call the 'English touch' – a combination of flair and quiet unassuming elegance – always remains, a touchstone and guide which can only be 'ours'.

NIGEL HAVERS

INTRODUCTION

Style transforms the man. It is elegant, witty, classic and ageless and makes up for lack of physical perfection in the way that 'grace' enhances a woman. It is also the downfall of those who fail to understand it.

Beloved by the British media in the Eighties, the word 'style' has been greatly misunderstood and misrepresented. It has become the mega-monosyllable which describes everything to which we aspire.

Meaning far more than fashion, 'style' is the contemporary answer to 'class'. It reflects the new economic equality in that it is available – potentially – to anyone. At its best, real English style remains an elusive quality to be craved and cultivated. At its worst, it is cheap imitation.

Much of contemporary 'style' is derived from images on television. As such, it reflects a wide and sometimes confusing outlook on life which is often removed from traditional realities. Young people today are 'style conscious' without understanding what the concept means. Young men, in particular, often assume that style is instantaneous, something to be put on the credit card along with the latest car. In fact, it is a process that grows with the individual.

There was a time not too long ago when the Englishman knew all about style. It came from a mixture of dress and behaviour and he learned the basic principles from his father. To these, he added his own individual touch and his style developed naturally. He did not need explanations. In time and with a little prompting, he simply 'knew'.

Society changes, and wisdom is no longer inherited. Today's wealth is won and lost in a moment. 'Success' is valued economically and 'style' has been falsely interpreted as the outward manifestation of money.

But as we move from the financially voracious Eighties towards an age more conscious of its debts, old values are beginning to return. There is a new appreciation of the classic appeal of clothes that endure the fluctuations of fashion. The traditional style of the Englishman, updated to suit a more 'international' world of constant travel and transatlantic business, is once more appreciated for its timeless worth. The English Style of Dress, for so long admired and imitated abroad, is once again enjoyed by its rightful wearer – the Englishman.

English style is a special blend of many contributing factors. It has historical roots and social implications but most of all, it is a real reflection of the peculiar character of its creator.

The Englishman has always enjoyed the role of reluctant star. He relishes the conflict between 'understatement' and an uninhibited love of 'dressing up'. No one is better at dressing for occasions than the traditional English gentleman. He will happily primp himself into 'special occasion' outfits that have their origin in Regency England and he continues to dress for a country weekend in the manner of an eighteenth-century squire. Yet the Englishman has a horror of anything 'outrageous' in either looks or behaviour and an inbuilt fear of appearing ridiculous.

For this reason, he tends to stick to 'uniform' (whether it is the safe uniform of a conventional suit or the exotic 'uniform' of the latest streetwise trend, or even Royal Ascot) because in uniform he feels safe.

Beside the usual social and psychological reasons (the influence of school uniform, the need to conform), there are historical reasons for this. Much of twentieth-century male fashion has been influenced by the uniform of warfare. The duffle coat, for example, first came into its own when it was adopted by the Royal Navy, and our military heritage is still seen in double-breasted coats, rough materials, patch pockets and the ubiquitous use of fawn, khaki and navy.

Before the First World War, European armies indulged their love of colour on the battlefield. They went to war in a spectacular display of tight-fitting and brightly coloured uniforms. Even in 1914, the Belgians and French were marching out in red and blue.

For the British, however, colonial bush wars had already shown that in skirmishes against the natives more subdued clothing was not only safer but more comfortable. Enterprising colonial officers who went native and adopted versions of the clothing and equipment of their adversaries early refuted the criticism that the Englishman cannot be inventive in his dress.

'Khaki' clothing was developed in the Colonies and later used for fighting wear in Europe. By the outbreak of the First World War, most European countries had adopted some kind of brown or grey camouflage. The male with the dun-coloured plumage was hatched into an equally grey world.

Britain's great contribution to Second World War uniform was battle dress. First introduced in 1937, it conformed to the contemporary criterion for many a male outfit by being uncomfortable and unsmart. But it was considered 'practical' as it was simple to make and the use of cloth was economical. For these reasons it was later copied by the Germans and the Americans (in 1944).

"The Englishman is lucky. He can draw on an excellent

uniform of good quality classics provided by traditional Jermyn

Street tailoring which gives his wardrobe an immediately

acceptable base. Once he has that, he can enjoy embellishing

with the details that spell out personal style."

PAUL KEERS, *Editor of British GQ*

The American influence soon made its mark in post-war Britain. The USA was confident and strong, its society more mobile and less rigid than the British.

Denim was the material of the moment and jeans were made popular by American film stars such as Marlon Brando and James Dean. The British held out against such casualness. In 1960, 'correct dress' at Oxford was cavalry twill trousers and a tweed jacket, but by the end of the decade the explosion in the university population had challenged the old authority and jeans and T-shirts became symbols of the new 'liberalism'.

In Britain, this meant Carnaby Street where in 1966 men's clothing boutiques outnumbered all others. The Beatles wore suits with velvet collars, and floral fabrics and frilly shirts indicated a new 'relaxed' attitude that was laid back to the point of inertia. The Seventies saw a brief return to army surplus introduced by the Vietnam war. Young men returned rebelliously to uniform but already the mood was changing in the light of new economic factors.

Rising unemployment made the scruffy and un-couth an unacceptable sign of being down and out. Suits became the badge of the new conservatism and Mrs Thatcher's Britain passed rapidly to a new materialism in which business, once regarded as a rather mundane affair, became not only acceptable but universally admired.

The Eighties have seen the meteoric rise of the 'upwardly mobile professional' and, in some cases, his equally swift decline. Once again the mood has subtly shifted from 'dynamic' and 'forward-looking' to a more sedate concern with tradition. Conservation now goes hand in hand with conservatism and 'consistency' is the key word of the age.

It is also the key word of style. It isn't just a question of matching each item of clothing or of immaculate grooming. Style is about being independently confident enough to allow a personal feeling to evolve and to show through in dress and manner wherever and whatever the circumstances. It is a true expression of yourself.

No book can tell a man precisely how to be himself, but, as with everything, good advice can sometimes help. Without advice, it is easy to settle for mediocrity, to stick safely to 'uniform' and go on looking like everyone else.

There's nothing wrong with uniform itself, provid-ing it suits your particular needs. It may be minimal or modern, merely affordable or pure luxury, designer-dedicated or classically conventional. It *must* be comfortable, it must make the wearer feel confident that he looks good and it must provide the background for those individual touches of style which mark out the man from the masses. In this day and age, these 'simple touches' can be the hardest to achieve.

In the past an Englishman's style came directly from being 'dressed in the best'. His clothing indicated social standing and economic prosperity and his knowledge of 'correct uniform' was passed down from father to son.

Several factors have contributed to diminish this 'traditional' sense of style in the British male, not least his changing role in society. Woman's new economic and social independence has reduced man's role as a 'provider' and increased her influence over his choice of clothes. The average young man-about-town of the Seventies and Eighties was too willing a victim to female designs on his body. He allowed himself to be shop-led through the High Street and permitted logos to become more important than line.

The Designer Label came to rule as the measure of Eighties elegance. A suit was no longer simply a suit, it was a Name which, in itself, was expected to guarantee instant change in the wearer's image. Clothes came to say less about the man who wore them than about the man who had designed them. 'Image' had less to do with a man's individuality than with a 'look' promoted by advertising in the glossy magazines. 'Style' itself was in danger of becoming uniform as the Yuppies exhibited more Cash than Dash in city clothing.

The contemporary Englishman has been somewhat battered by the storm. In general a discerning sort of chap, he has lately taken to 'projecting' himself without subtlety. His worst fault perhaps has been his unwillingness to ask questions about clothes, grooming, behaviour, or any other subject which in the past has been considered frivolous, irrelevant or received wisdom. Faced with a sudden dramatic breadth of choice and seemingly endless options, he has floundered in his eagerness to create the right image – and all too often has settled for the wrong one.

This book, therefore, is for any man who feels he could benefit from a little discreet advice on 'appearance'. It is as much for the seemingly self-possessed who simply wants to know how to adopt a more rational approach to clothes as for the young man who stutters over the condom counter and collects clothes based on image rather than necessity or logic. It offers an outline on well-balanced dressing with a long-term approach which is not only stylish but economical. It also gives hints on all-important details which turn fashion into individuality and, because style is to do with the 'whole' man, it offers advice on grooming and behaviour.

Each man has his own 'style'. To some it comes more naturally, born of a confidence which others have to learn. That it *can* be learnt is without question.

The discerning man will use the information here to adopt and adapt whatever he personally needs. In the process, he will perhaps come closer to the concept of the English gentleman, the ageless and quintessentially British character whose appeal is international and whose style, modelled on the confirmed wisdom of tradition, is the envy of everyone.

CHAPTER ONE

THE ENGLISHMAN'S WARDROBE

"Whenever anyone says 'style' to me, I immediately
think of sexual behaviour."

ALAN COREN

Dress style does not need a large budget. Nor does it rely on indulging in the 'escapism' introduced by fringe fashion, especially in times of recession. Men rarely feel the same need as women to alter their image according to each season's fashion convention but instead, they err in the opposite direction, by hardly altering it at all.

Men are adept at the 'capsule' wardrobe if this means the collection of a few items which have been lovingly worn and torn for years. For a man, the usual interpretation of 'long-term investment' in clothing is not something which will usefully see him through a variety of occasions but a garment he has grown up in.

A man can afford to settle for less fashion and more first-class quality. He can build himself a limited background on which to add an unlimited amount of colour and the detailed touches of 'surprise' which are the keynotes of style. But first, he must decide on his priorities.

It is useless to have one suit if you never wear it. Equally useless to have a suede or leather jacket as the most expensive and luxurious item in your wardrobe if you work in an office where suits are mandatory.

Begin by looking at the items of clothing you have which you wear most and try to decide why you like them. Are they comfortable? Is the colour good, do you feel 'right'? These are all valid reasons but instantly discard anything that you cling to for sentiment – like dated bell-bottomed trousers or a grease-stained old school tie.

Next, consider your own lifestyle and decide on the essentials that your way of life dictates. Are you the British Council type with corduroy suits and Fair-Isle pullovers, the Bank Manager type in sensible chainstore suits with starched shirt, the Pinstripe type, traditional values occasionally updated with matching tie and handkerchief set, the Military type who signals to other men with his regimental tie, the Fashion Fanatic dressed in perpetual black, the Media-man with the dripdry shirt or the Berkeley Square type whose gravel-patch kneecaps reveal too many nights spent falling out of nightclubs and into gutters?

The ingredients of a good 'basic' wardrobe should all work together. They should cover most eventualities and for the Englishman in particular, it is important that they should cover most seasons. The British climate doesn't allow for too much distinction between summer and winter and in any case, for clothes to give maximum versatility, they should be as classic, timeless and as 'cross-season' as possible. So think first of materials that can be worn all year – light wools, cottons, corduroy and, if affordable, cashmere and silk.

SUITS

Men remember their first suits like women recall their first loves. In both cases it's worth looking beyond mere appearances for practicality and usefulness. A suit is likely to be one of the most expensive items in your wardrobe so first consider whether you really need it. If you do, determine to buy the best you can afford. Suits are not an emblem of style in themselves. A suit symbolises a degree of formality but style does not rely on being formal. Even so, a well-cut suit of good quality material certainly *does* have style and it is worth taking time over selection. The next chapter deals with suits in detail but note the following in advance.

Never buy a suit which does not fit properly. Most ready-made suits are fashioned for the 'average' figure and do not take into account such common defects as one shoulder higher or one leg longer than the other. When buying off-the-peg, always look for a generous cut. Avoid jackets which are tight across the back or under the arms. Look for trousers that come right up to the waist and don't stop at the hips or beneath the stomach. Choose the best material you can afford, preferably a pure wool worsted which will wear well. Check the details: are buttons sewn on tightly? any loose threads at the seams? Look for good points which distinguish a really well-made jacket: a well-cut collar that is soft and lies flat, buttons hand sewn for extra strength, cuff buttons (three or four) which unfasten.

Remember the three essentials of buying a suit: Cut, Cloth and Comfort, the greatest of which is comfort. Make sure you really move in the outfit before purchasing – sit, walk, stretch, bend. It sounds obvious but the natural tendency is simply to stand still in front of a mirror.

Don't be tempted by anything unusual in colour. Play safe with grey or navy blue and rely on other details such as ties and pocket handkerchiefs to provide colour interest.

Finally, do not be led by the label. No garment can transform the wearer by its label alone. It should never say more about the designer than it does about you.

Shirts

Probably the most important item in a man's wardrobe is a plain white shirt in softest sea-island cotton. If you can afford to purchase only one luxury item, then buy this. Make sure that it is 'Jermyn Street quality', that is, 100 per cent cotton or two-fold poplin with double cuffs, mother-of-pearl buttons, generous tails and fine stitching around the collar, preferably with removable collar stays. It should also be 'optical white', not cream or yellowing, and very soft, not 'crisp'. The soft white shirt is *the* element of style to suit any occasion. It looks just as well worn with blue jeans, with sleeves rolled up and collar left open (with or without accompanying blazer or tweed jacket) as it does neatly buttoned and 'tied' under a city suit.

Men today make the same mistakes with shirts that women traditionally make with hats. They regard them as inexpensive enough to ring the changes on an outfit and the one area in which they can afford to experiment with style and colour. Hence the phenomenon of British politicians wearing red shirts (first worn by Garibaldi in the 1860s) and bright stripes or checks which 'shout' against the sombre background of a dark city suit. Coloured shirts are fine as long as they are worn with a sense of proportion. Stick to pastels and fine stripes for wear with suits and keep bold colours or patterns for more casual clothes when they can be counterbalanced with a coloured sweater, trousers, socks, scarves and other accessories.

Before buying, check collar size regularly to account for any weight change by measuring the neck around the Adam's apple and adding half an inch to the reading on the tape-measure. Shirts make good sale bargains provided you buy from an outlet you know you can trust or from a manufacturer renowned for top quality. Never be tempted to buy a selection just because they seem inexpensive.

Colour and collar-shape on shirts are important for each individual as this item of clothing is so close to the face. A pink shirt, for example, can look drastic against a very florid

THE ESSENTIAL (WHITE) SHIRT IS
SOFTEST SEA-ISLAND COTTON AND A
CRISPNESS CORRECT IN TELESCOPIC
DETAIL.

complexion. Long narrow collars tend to accentuate long narrow faces and prim rounded collars can make a plump face look even fuller. Some men worry a great deal about sleeve length. It does not need to be 'inch perfect' (an inch below the jacket sleeve) but long cuffs can dwarf small hands and short cuffs emphasise large hands.

The number of shirts you need depends on where and how you work. Office workers need a change of shirt every day. Cities are notoriously grimy places and no shirt can look smart with a grubby collar and cuffs. Most men today own more shirts than they need, many of which are hardly worn because once out of the cellophane, they disappoint. A good white shirt will never let you down like this.

JACKETS

If suits are not the main feature of your wardrobe, choose good quality separates that provide a co-ordinating link. Jackets must be a really good fit and the style and colour as neutral as possible if the garment is to be versatile but not boring. Styles and shape of jacket are almost endless so it may help to think of three main types: semi-formal, casual and country.

THE SEMI-FORMAL JACKET. The blazer is probably the most useful semi-formal jacket a man can own. The shape of the blazer has been copied and re-vamped as a 'loose, unstructured jacket' and sometimes appears in checks and stripes, especially in the cotton variety. Better to avoid all this and go straight for the classic tailored shape in pure lightweight navy wool.

Once again, check the details. The classic blazer has all the hallmarks of top quality. The lapels are 'rolled' so that they lie evenly against the jacket instead of being pressed stiffly flat. The pockets are 'jetted' and 'flapped'. In other words, they have a neat double seam which allows the flap to be worn tucked in or out of the pocket. The jacket should be fully lined to help retain its shape. Finally, an important 'style' note: choose buttons that are either plain or have the most discreet decoration possible. Avoid anything that is nautical, brassy, ostentatiously 'logoed' or has a badge on the pocket. The blazer should be a background for your own individual style and therefore as plain as possible.

(ABOVE) COOLER VERSION OF THE
INDISPENSABLE WHITE SHIRT.
(BELOW) A BIT OF A SILLY DOT.

TAKE A LONG HARD LOOK AT YOURSELF
AND DECIDE THE IMAGE YOU WANT TO
PROJECT. AVOID IMITATION. EXAMINE
THE MOULD, THEN BREAK IT.

Do try and invest in the best. If the jacket is to be a major item in your wardrobe, it is worth spending more. The versatility of the blazer will certainly repay the outlay. Worn with a white shirt, tie and grey flannels, the blazer instantly becomes the 'uniform' of the semi-formally dressed gentleman. Worn with a cashmere or wool polo-neck pullover and fine cord trousers or khaki 'chinos', it becomes elegantly casual. For this is the blazer's forte – it always looks well dressed, even worn with an open-necked shirt and a pair of denim jeans, and has an unbeatable air of elegance.

Add your own touch of style to a formal look with accessories (*see Chapter 6*) but keep it simple. The secret of style is an unstudied appearance. The more effortless and unrehearsed it seems, the more stylish it becomes. Keep a sense of proportion. Ties and pocket handkerchiefs look odd with jeans and sneakers – the top half becomes more formal and 'contrived' than the bottom.

THE RELAXED LEATHER LOUCHE.

THE CASUAL JACKET. Really casual jackets are those which never attempt to look formal and are more often worn with sweaters than with shirts. Leather and suede come into this category and once again it pays to buy the best. The majority of leathers fall into four main groups: lamb, cow, sheep and pig. Cowhide is the least expensive and is easy to shape by various techniques which include 'pressing' and 'painting'. The cheaper variety often has animal scars or marks which are spray painted by the manufacturer which leaves the skin coarse textured.

Always choose the softest leather possible. A really good skin can be judged by its 'feel'. The softer and more supple it feels to the touch, the better it is – and usually, the more expensive. Lambskin tops the price range and the best comes from France, New Zealand and Great Britain. Good quality leathers wear well as they seem to take on 'character' with age, a style-note in itself. Suede is different. It marks more easily and requires regular professional cleaning though the occasional dusting down with a small amount of talcum powder will help. There's nothing 'stylish' about a greasy collar on a suede jacket and it is better to avoid anything fringed, or heavily punch-patterned which dates rapidly.

Suede and leather probably do not feature at all in the wardrobe of the City man or office worker. But for many a male with a more 'casual' approach to professional dressing they provide a casual style which goes well with the 'jeans and T-shirt' look. Simplicity is vital. Don't try to 'dress up' suede or leather with shirts, ties or Flying Ace scarves and hats. Leave it casual and unexaggerated and if you cannot afford to keep suede and leather clean, don't buy it.

THE COUNTRY CASUAL JACKET. The tweed jacket is a hallmark of country style and was once the favourite mufti of the military man. The heavy Harris or Donegal tweed has become caricatured as the 'style' of retired British Colonels living in Dorset but in recent years, Continental designers have taken tweed and re-fashioned it into garments of an altogether softer and more elegant style which now suits both country and town life. Heavy tweed comes into its own on the grouse moors (*see Chapter 4*) but the 'shapely' Continental-styled jacket in a lighter material will be more generally useful. It will look equally well-balanced in town with a lightweight sweater, jeans and sneakers as in the country teamed more traditionally with heavy pullover, cords and wellington boots.

Look for a generous cut under the arms as this jacket will probably be worn with a sweater and need extra room for movement. Be more adventurous with choice of colour. Tweed now comes in a wide range of heather blues and greens which are softer and more subtle than traditional brown. If the jacket is to be worn mainly in town and only for occasional country weekends, choose a more 'refined' wool and cashmere mix of material which will combine country casualness with town 'style' and give you two jackets for the price of one. Once again, reach for the best – good material, well cut and comfortable.

No one can dictate which of these three styles is best for you. It may be that all or none of them are, but whichever type of jacket you choose, make sure it's more than just a top layer. It should team in with the rest of your wardrobe and to do so, it should be devoid of exaggerated 'fashion' notes. Length, shape, style are personal choices but in general it's best to keep it plain. This way, the jacket is most likely to serve a year-round purpose and really work as a 'basic' garment.

TROUSERS

Cut and fit are crucial, whatever the fashion. Some men prefer to buy a suit with two pairs of trousers because they feel the trousers will wear more quickly than the jacket. In fact, this depends on the quality of the material and how it is treated. Too much gutter-grovelling at four in the morning results in a diseased state of the knees called 'gravel patching'. Then there is 'chauffeur's bum' and 'hamster's pocket' to contend with.

Good trousers are half-lined to ensure they hang properly. This also makes them more comfortable and helps prolong their life. Choose material that wears well – wool, for example, or cotton in summer. Natural wool is a hard-wearing material and does not necessarily need to be mixed with man-made fibres. Cotton is cool for summer but light wool with a small percentage of polyester will crease less. Wear corduroy, denim and flannel for leisure. They are good all-season fabrics. Keep heavy tweed or gaberdine for winter wear.

COCKTAILS ON DECK CLASSIC, LOOSE
FITTING JACKET AND COMFORTABLE
TROUSERS – A RELAXED WAY TO SINK
THE GIN.

A belt is not regulation wear with trousers though some men feel in danger without one. Trousers with pleats from the waist look better without belts and are often more comfortable to wear as they allow additional room for movement. Braces are acceptable provided they are the button, *not* the clip variety. Avoid red elastic as being very dated Wall Street and rather secondary modern.

Check that side pockets on trousers are deep, not only for practicality but because it makes for a smoother line. Button flies are traditional but time-consuming. Zips suit the faster pace of office life but should always be taken right up and tucked into the fold in the fabric.

TIES

Ties are rightly considered more than mere accessories. Most men own a collection, some of which are rarely worn but never discarded. It is better to have a dozen top-quality silk ties than an ill assortment.

Amongst your tie collection should be a black silk-knit. Much maligned for its lack of originality, the black silk-knit can still see a man through a variety of occasions from formal to funeral.

Choose at least one other tie in traditional 'regimental' stripes but give careful thought to the institutional tie. The idea that the man who wears his colours on his chest is somehow suspicious only applies if he is wearing the tie of an institution to which he does not belong or if he is wearing the tie of an institution to which he should not need to proclaim that he belongs. It is far more stylish to wear proudly the tie of the Bingley Bricklaying Society or the Australian Cork Conservationists than to wear an institutional tie which everyone instantly recognises.

Other ties in a man's collection should include plain and patterned silks in rich colours (pastels 'wash' into the background of a plain shirt front) and at least one silk scarf as this is an understated accessory of great importance since it works as well with evening dress as with an open-neck shirt (*see Chapter 6 for details on how to wear it*).

Always buy the best in ties. Look for those which are hand finished, made of three pieces of material all cut on the bias, and avoid all but the most discreet initials if they

belong to people other than yourself. Ties should be regularly dry-cleaned as nothing is less stylish than a tie which is greasy, spotted or creased. Always tie carefully, not pulling the knot too tight, and positioning it exactly between the points of the collar. Undo the knot completely before removing a tie. Hang it or roll it, end to end, smoothing out any creases, and keep in a shallow drawer.

SHOES

Every man's wardrobe should have at least two pairs of plain black Oxfords and those who work in town should own

COMFORT IS THE MOST IMPORTANT
ELEMENT IN FOOTWEAR. CHOOSE A
WARM SOCK THAT COMPLETELY COVERS
THE GAP BETWEEN FOOTWEAR AND
TROUSER BOTTOM AND A WELL-FITTING
SHOE TO BOOT.

many more. The all-leather Oxford performs both day and evening and provides good support for the man who is frequently on his feet.

Ready-made shoes have improved enormously but if you have awkward feet (and who hasn't?) it may well be worth investigating custom-made shoes. The process of making them (in London, where it is a particular art) is usually long, between three and six months, and because of the amount of work and the use of only the best materials, the product will not be inexpensive. But as quality ready-made shoes can also be very costly these days, it is worth considering paying the price of a pair of custom-made shoes. They may be a better investment.

When buying ready-made always choose all-leather. The Germans make the best upper calf in the world followed by the Swiss and the French. Italian and Spanish leather shoes follow seasonal fashion changes and this is worth bearing in mind if you have shoes made abroad. Slip-on shoes are less supportive to the feet and it is better to avoid those with tassels, bits and buckles which are sometimes difficult to clean, in favour of the plainer Pennyloafer. Brogues are rather heavy going in town and the half-brogue is a better choice. Sneakers, trainers or plain plimsolls do nothing to support the feet and can add to problems like foot odour. There is nothing stylish about a battered pair of plimsolls which look as if they were breakfasted on by mice.

Even top quality leather shoes cannot look elegant if they are not kept well heeled and polished. Debrett's book, *The English Gentleman*, whimsically suggests that a gentleman's shoes should be 'polished with ox blood' which is a similar eccentricity to 'washing his riding breeches in urine' but today's young gentleman can probably manage with a good wax and the spit-and-polish 'army' method (spitting on the wax helps work it into the shoe). Keep shoes in racks in the bottom of the wardrobe and use wooden shoe trees as they will help keep leather in shape.

COATS

Heated offices and travel to and from work by public or private transport have reduced the role of the coat as an essential item. Coats call for considerable financial outlay and to justify their purchase, should be in use for at least half the year.

If you decide you need one, choose a coat that is traditionally styled – a double-breasted classic with well-proportioned collar made in heavy wool or tweed. Avoid the 'fashion' garment with fur collar and acres of materials whose shape diminishes all but those more than seven feet tall.

Choose a length that comes to the back of the knee. Anything shorter gets crumpled when sitting down. For the same reason, avoid a single back vent which reaches to the back thighs. Single vents are unkind to the man with a portly stomach and a large behind, especially if he likes to place his hands in his pockets. The result is to draw the coat tightly across the body, leaving the rear exposed.

Navy and camel are traditionally popular for town coats but, in fact, neither is particularly practical as these

THE ALL-PURPOSE,
STONE-COLOURED MACKINTOSH
– SIMPLE IN LINE AND STYLE.

colours quickly show marks and dirt. Cashmere is also popular, though not the best material for a garment which is often expected to work hard. Cashmere is a luxury fabric and a pure cashmere coat is not designed for tough wear. If this is to be the only coat in your wardrobe, choose something which works as well in the country as in town. The Austrian Loden is a good 'international' classic which fits this demanding role. (*For more on the subject see Chapter 3.*)

Another good alternative is a raincoat with a detachable lining. Choose the traditional trench shape which seems to take on character with age. But the classic stone colour needs frequent dry-cleaning. There is nothing stylish about any garment which is grubby or soiled.

SWEATERS

Sweaters are an important feature of the male wardrobe not only for their intrinsic practicality but because they provide the opportunity for legitimate use of colour. Years of association with standard army green, naval blue, neutral arrans and rather faded Fair-Isles have left the average Englishman wisely impervious to 'colour counselling'. However, the use of colour in a small wardrobe can greatly add to its versatility.

"Men tend to think in terms of solid colours meaning putting the green shirt with the green sweater etc. It's better to think in shades – the bottle green shirt 'blended' with the olive jacket for example. total colour coordination can mean you end up looking like wallpaper."
KAFFE FASSETT *('Mr Knitting')*

As most of a man's clothes will be 'neutral', the occasional vivid sweater can 'lift' an entire look – the best plan is to experiment and discover what works well for you. Colour is an individual matter and very dependent on different skin and hair types but the following general guidelines will help.

If your skin is pale, go for positive complementary colours, avoid pale tones. Those with fair or grey hair should resist light shades of tan, grey or yellow as too self-effacing. Olive skin types with dark hair should avoid the paler pinks or greys and choose clear blue or red and navy. Red-haired men look best in basic neutrals – charcoal brown, khaki and navy and should obviously avoid pinks and bright red.

Choose sweaters made from lambswool, shetland, cashmere and cotton. If you can afford only one luxury, make it a V-necked cable-stitched classic four-ply cashmere in cream. Like the soft white shirt, it will work with almost anything.

Sweater shape is also important (*see Chapter 3*), depending on height and build. So is cleaning. Regular washing or dry-cleaning will not only keep sweaters in shape but will prolong their life. Never drag a sweater up over your head by grabbing a handful at the middle of the back. Remember to fold or hang your sweater up when you take it off.

UNDERWEAR

The item of clothing a man puts on first and considers last, underwear is important because what goes underneath can affect the line of clothes that lie on top. The Englishman has always favoured the 'baggy' brief, which may account for the success hitherto of the boxer short. But any idea that the sudden flowering of prints and patterns in the male underworld is a novelty can be soon dismissed. Union-Jack-decorated underwear was made popular at the coronation of George V, long before it was flourished from the football terraces.

Good underwear is made in a material which breathes – cotton, silk or a light thermal fabric and never in nylon. Don't wear tight briefs: they are not only uncomfortable and a potential health risk but leave an unattractive line beneath trousers. Underwear should be worn but not seen – only mad Continentals strip to their vests in summer and the words Y-front should never appear publicly on sagging elastic like a rearguard cry for help. String vests are rarely a thing of beauty and should never be visible beneath a shirt front.

CARING FOR CLOTHES

Whatever you have in your wardrobe, it will be much improved and give you much better style value if it is kept clean and in good repair. 'Kit inspection' should begin before you purchase. Always read labels carefully and if the item

BOXER SHORTS WERE A DEFINITE STEP
UP ON THE BAGGY Y-FRONT BUT
WHATEVER YOUR UNDERCOVER, KEEP
IT CLEAN, COTTON AND COMFORTABLE.

requires more loving care and attention than you can possibly give it, think twice about buying.

Ironing is not a favourite male occupation but shirts must be well pressed if they are to look good. Don't use a very hot iron and keep shirts hung on contoured hangers if possible, as this helps minimise creases better than folding. Cotton shirts are always better laundered than dry-cleaned. Don't be tempted to douse shirts with sodawater or scrub at spots as this damages silk and may cause colours to 'bleed'.

Blot any stains on ties and dry-clean as soon as possible. Dry-cleaning a tie is a difficult business which usually involves disassembling the item so choose your tradesman with care.

Always hang jackets and trousers on shaped and padded hangers (most good retailers supply these with purchase) and don't crush them in a cupboard. Trousers retain shape best when hung vertically rather than folded over a hanger. Trouser presses can help but not if they are used in place of regular dry-cleaning. This has the same effect as ironing 'tired' trousers; it 'cooks' the dirt into the fabric and helps destroy it.

Brush clothes regularly to remove surface dirt and remember that specialist materials such as suede and leather require specialist treatment. Raincoats will also need re-proofing from time to time as dry-cleaning solvents can remove their water repellency.

Always bear in mind that the details help create the whole picture. The man with holes in his socks (if you don't know how to darn them ask a local tailor who may do it as part of his 'alteration' service) cannot hope to compensate with an expensive suit and will always lose out to the colleague who has taken the trouble to look spruce, clean and therefore elegant.

THE BASIC 'BASICS'

How many suits or shirts you need will be dictated by your personal lifestyle. However, it may help to organise things by thinking in terms of a Travel Checklist. Apart from a ravishing blonde and a bottle of whisky, the following items could usefully accompany you on a business trip.

THREE SUITS, TWO IN MID-GREY FLANNEL OR LIGHTWEIGHT WOOL, ONE DARK NAVY. WEAR THE GREY FOR DAY, KEEP THE DARK BLUE FOR EVENING OR TO CREATE A MORE FORMAL IMPRESSION.

SIX SOFT WHITE COTTON SHIRTS, TWO PALE BLUE IN *FIL À FIL* (END TO END), TWO FINE-STRIPED. KEEP THE BLUE AND STRIPED SHIRTS FOR OFFICE WEAR, INTERCHANGED WITH A WHITE SHIRT WHICH CAN ALSO BE ADAPTED FOR EVENING OR MORE CASUAL OCCASIONS.

ONE DOUBLE-BREASTED (MORE FORMAL) DARK NAVY BLUE LIGHTWEIGHT WOOL BLAZER AND ONE PAIR OF DARK FLANNELS – SAFE FOR ALMOST EVERY OCCASION FROM COCKTAILS TO CONFERENCES AND THE BEST BET FOR LESS FORMAL WEEKEND DINNERS – ALTERNATE WITH A PAIR OF FINE CORDUROY TROUSERS FOR MORE INFORMAL WEEKEND WEAR.

ONE V-NECK, CABLE-STITCHED SWEATER IN FOUR-PLY CASHMERE, COLOUR OPTIONAL ALTHOUGH CREAM PROVIDES THE MOST VERSATILE BACKGROUND. WEAR WITH THE FLANNELS AND THE CORDS.

ONE TRADITIONALLY TRENCH-STYLED RAINCOAT WITH DETACHABLE LINING.

TWO PAIRS OF BLACK OXFORDS AND ONE PAIR OF BLACK LOAFERS.

A SELECTION OF TIES INCLUDING ONE BLACK SILK-KNIT.

A SELECTION OF SOCKS IN NAVY, BLACK AND DARK GREY.

CHAPTER TWO

THE ENGLISHMAN'S SUIT

"City style should never be complicated or flashy. Clothes should be unfussy, immaculate and well cared for. I don't dress to cause comment but to look smart."

VISCOUNT ALTHORP

A good suit is a sign of establishment. It denotes confidence, sophistication and social status. In the climate of the new conservatism it has become the uniform of success and its rise in significance has paralleled the economic difference between the employed and the jobless.

The British suit has set the standard for correct dress worldwide and many would agree with costume historian Diane de Marly that it is 'the true mark of civilisation and sophistication'. It is also a 'uniform' which instantly stands or falls by the distinction of its cut and cloth, which in turn reflects the style of the man who wears it.

A traditional suit is a very imposing outfit and for that reason not everyone feels at ease in one. Continental influence has softened the line and made the suit a more relaxed and acceptable outfit for the young, though only a few can afford the glamour of high fashion.

For most men, a suit remains a necessary part of working life, chosen for its conformity. The man with style will begin by looking beyond this for a suit that inspires confidence when he wants to impress and which, chosen well, will be an investment in projecting a positive image that will soon repay its price.

There are still two main ways to buy a suit. You can either have it tailored for you individually, or you can purchase it ready-made. Nowadays, there is a wide area of choice between these two simple cases of 'how' and 'where'.

You may, for example choose a Savile Row or a city tailor who is renowned for traditionally styled suits. This is a good place to start if you want a suit that carries 'weight' (quite literally in some cases, as the wool-weight of material is important). Or, if you are looking for something a little less imposing but still bearing most of the hallmarks of a traditionally 'tailored' suit, you may choose one of the new, specialist suit shops where you can have a suit 'made to order'. (This differs from made-to-measure in that a standard suit is ordered and tailored round a basic stock size.) You may buy your off-the-peg suit from a chainstore, a department store, a shop specialising in traditional English style (new or second-hand), another selling elegant Italian or French suits, or even by mail order.

There are advantages to all, as the Englishman who

THE RIGHT FABRIC TO MAKE A SUIT IS
INFLUENCED BY TEXTURE AND WEIGHT
AS WELL AS COLOUR CHOICE.
MATERIALS ALSO VARY BUT WOOL IS
ONE OF THE MOST VERSATILE.

once slavishly made his way into business on the balance of his father's Prince of Wales check is at last beginning to appreciate, but whichever you choose, the importance of Cut, Cloth and Comfort, as mentioned before, are fundamental. Only a correct combination of these is sufficient to give a man the confidence he needs to wear a suit with style. A suit must fit the man: the man should never be expected to fit the suit.

Cloth has played an important part in the history of the tailored British suit since it first made its appearance in England (round about the seventeenth century). Wool, once the cloth of the ordinary man, responded well to the craft of tailoring, as it could be more easily shaped and handled than fine fabrics like silk with a more variable weave. Wool is still one of the most versatile and practical materials for a city suit.

THE CITY SUIT – STREET CRED. FOR THE
MARKET MAKERS. NOTE THE
NAPOLEONIC STANCE WHICH HINTS AT
EURO- STYLE.

The cut of the long jacket of the seventeenth-century suit heralded the style of the frock coat which remained the model for the well-dressed man-about-town until after the First World War. The 'lounge suit' was considered very casual as its name suggests – an outfit only suitable for country wear. Polite society rejected its use in town until Edward, Prince of Wales wore a short jacket and turn-up trousers during his tour of Canada in 1919. This event first made the lounge suit fashionable.

Long before the influence of Mrs Simpson, the Duke of Windsor had shown a dislike of the formality preferred by his father, George V. He was a great champion of comfortable clothes and he gave the royal approval to a variety of 'casual' garments for daily wear including soft, turn-down collars and trilby hats.

The current Prince of Wales is conventional in his approach and seems to emulate the style of the Duke of Edinburgh in his choice of superbly cut suits. Those fortunate enough to have seen a royal suit at close quarters will have observed the excellence of the cut and material and also noted that the weave is sometimes 'personalised' by a pinstripe constructed from tiny initials: a stylish royal detail which elevates the 'man of letters' beyond the realms of the ordinary logo.

The present Duke of York favours double-breasted suits. Perhaps they remind him of naval uniform but in any case, they are more flattering to larger men of portly girth. Prince Edward generally chooses more relaxed single-breasted suits in lighter material and lighter shade to those favoured by his elder brothers. However, like all the men of the British royal family, he always look impeccably dressed in suits which would never presume to superimpose another personality on the wearer.

Not so with many of the 'fashion' suits of today. No one would deny that the designer suit has contributed a great deal to menswear. The popularity of various Continental names such as Armani, Versace and Gaultier has not only increased interest in fashion amongst the young but has helped focus attention on design detail which previously existed in forlorn obscurity. Giorgio Armani, for example, took the traditional shape of the blazer and turned it into a garment which was altogether softer. The American designer Ralph

Lauren has also reworked traditional materials, such as tweeds, in a way that is wearable and new.

As such, the great designers of the Seventies and Eighties have offered valuable inspiration to menswear. But as with all fashion input, how much the individual gets from this depends on how and why he chooses to interpret it.

He can approach the subject rationally with a relaxed, independent attitude of mind and turn a fashion trend to his own advantage. Or he can simply absorb the latest look without considering whether he genuinely likes it or if it suits his particular style.

The real danger lies in doing nothing. On the question of suits, more than in any other area of his wardrobe, the Englishman has a tendency to dismiss the entire subject of changing trends. True, there are the brave few who move with the fashionable times, but the majority stay safely encased in suits which they honestly expect to see them through to retirement.

The result is a conformity (and often an aversion to suits) which conflicts with a secret longing for something a little different to brighten the dull routine of the white-collar worker's life.

The answer is simple. It lies in updating classic style and reworking it to combine the best of the old with a touch of the new. Fortunately, the Eighties has produced a 'new wave' of young designers, many of them British, who understand this perfectly and who have offered a solution with specialist retailing which combines traditional quality with a sense of fashion timing. In the process, they have helped give the impetus to the larger retailer whose expansion in the High Street has produced a choice which can sometimes border on the bewildering.

The following guidelines on tailor-made versus ready-to-wear should help clear some of the confusion but before deciding how or where to buy your suit consider a

THROUGH A GLASS BARCLAYS:
MANAGERIAL STYLE THAT LOOKS SOLID
AND CONFIDENT.

small amount of 'shopping logic'. Why do you need the suit? When will you wear it? How long do you want it to last? These are important questions that should be considered before purchase. Thereafter, choice becomes honed down more precisely to details of colour, material, pattern, shape and design.

The Tailor-made Suit

London's reputation for fine tailoring has established the well-cut British suit internationally and, in the past, the expectations an English gentleman had of his tailor mirrored his sense of moral standards: a sense of perfect proportion without any hint of extremes.

The best tailor-made suits still reflect character. They never look 'new' and are distinguished by their attention to detail which makes them an extension of the individual wearer. However, it should be borne in mind that most traditional tailoring is just that – traditional. No doubt a good tailor can fashion anything you require but if you are looking for the avant-garde, it is probably best not to start here.

"Clothes should never be tight as there is nothing elegant about tight jackets and trousers. A suit jacket should have plenty of room across the chest so that the cloth is not strained in any way."
HARDY AMIES

Once upon a time, young men were introduced to their tailors by their fathers. No doubt, this is sometimes still the case but many young men in business have made their way today on their own merits and for them in particular, the first rule in choosing a tailor is never to be afraid to ask questions. Good tailoring prides itself on a tradition of personal service. It is up to you, the customer, to take full advantage of this.

One of the major *dis*advantages of having a suit made is that you cannot possibly tell what it will be like until it is almost finished. It is essential therefore that you help the tailor by stating clearly at the very start, what it is you want.

Some of the questions you need to ask yourself are:

- Do you spend much time sitting in a car which may affect the number of extra pairs of trousers you need?

- Do you work under pressure and need extra room in your jacket, or do you always take your jacket off at work (and must therefore expect trousers to wear more quickly)?

- Do you frequently travel to other countries and need a suit in a weight of wool (or perhaps with a blend of man-made fibre) which will adapt to other climates and also travel well?

- Do you lose or gain weight easily?

- How many pockets do you need?

- What style of trousers (pleated at the waist? with turn-ups?) and jacket (one or two vents at the back?) do you usually wear and which do you find most comfortable?

- How often do you expect to wear it?

- Do you want a 'serious' business suit, or a suit which will also work less formally?

- How long do you realistically want the suit to last? (Good tailor-made suits are known for their longevity which obviously affects the amount of 'fashion' detail you will wish to include.)

Tailor-made suits were traditionally made to 'endure' and to act as their own central heating systems. They were usually cut from nineteen-ounce wool which was heavy compared with today's more common weight of between eleven and sixteen ounces. Wool is a very adaptable material and can even be used for 'tropical' suits. The fine smooth yarn of worsted is ideal for city suits as it is resilient and drapes well. The belief that wool should contain man-made fibre to make it hard-wearing is only really true of lightweight suits.

As times change, some tailors have introduced modern methods, including laser cutting. The traditionalists maintain that cutting by hand is still the best method and are prepared to take time over hand finishing so don't expect a classic custom-made suit in a hurry – some up-market tailors will take from three to six months to complete the process.

A good tailor guarantees his suits for at least a year and marks the date of purchase inside the jacket along with his name. He should be willing to make minor repairs and adjustments though a good suit will move 'in and out' with its wearer. Some tailors claim that the customer can lose or gain up to two stone before the suit will no longer accommodate them.

Make sure you feel comfortable in the suit when you go for the final fitting. Don't be afraid to stretch and move about and to ask for any alteration that seems necessary. Tailor-made suits are expensive, so demand value for your money. In return, you can expect a garment that will fit perfectly, that will be as comfortable as a second skin and should give good wear and be an acceptable classic in any climate or conditions for many years.

The Ready-made Suit

Nowadays, the simple heading of ready-made covers a wide variety of choice and where you buy your suits not only reflects how much you can be expected to pay, but what sort of assistance you can hope for.

As noted, one of the great benefits of traditional tailoring is the element of personal service involved. If you buy your suits ready-made in a chainstore, you will probably find that the 'service' is restricted to the business of taking your money.

This is fine if you know what you want but if in doubt, it is probably better to begin elsewhere. Most large department stores train their staff to give advice when it is required and usually offer an alteration service, but if you really want to benefit from sales knowledge you should go to a specialist shop.

This is undoubtedly the best half-way house between custom tailoring and off-the-peg. The customer has the advantage of inspecting the 'complete' article, of making

THE TRADITIONAL CITY SUIT BLENDS
INTO THE BACKGROUND. TAILOR-MADE
FOR DISTINCTION, UNIFORM,
CONVENTIONAL, FEW SURPRISES.

the purchase in much less time than would usually be required at a tailor's, and of having the garment 'finished' to suit his particular taste. A good specialist shop will gladly change buttons for you, make extra button holes and pockets and add other personal details as well as do all the usual adjustments of trouser and sleeve length. The clothes will be hand finished, the quality of material excellent and the price almost as much (sometimes more) than tailor-made. Although they will be traditionally cut, the clothes will already have that twist of style which makes a classic 'modern'.

Most specialist shops have more than one branch and many also offer a mail-order service so you may find what you want in Nottingham as easily as in London (where Covent Garden is now a close rival to Jermyn Street).

The large city-based department store is good for browsing and picking up tips on a variety of styles and manufacturers. Buyers from these stores attend the major fashion collections in Paris, London, New York and Milan and the clothes they select always contain at least some element of the very latest fashion. Top menswear department buyers advise customers always to wear proper shoes when buying a suit as this can affect the length of the trousers, to be open-minded about style, to ask for advice if necessary and not to take along a wife or girlfriend whose opinion may prejudice *your* personal choice.

The disadvantage of such a wide selection is that it can sometimes drive the customer back in confusion so that he settles for something 'safe'. Unfamiliarity breeds restraint, which is illustrated by the fact that the single-breasted navy blue suit still accounts for the largest percentage of High Street sales.

The chainstore also offers a wide variety of choice, though here the customer will find fewer individual fashion elements and a much wider degree of uniformity than anywhere else. The tendency is to sell more than the suit and promote a 'complete' look which leaves little room for imagination. In this case, style can become pre-packaged and it takes a strong character to resist the sale of a particular 'look' in favour of his own 'natural' selection.

Ready-made suits are produced to standard sizes but few men are 'average' shape. One hip higher than the other, sloping shoulders, short legs are all common problems. However, most menswear shops offer a variety of jacket fittings and trouser lengths but if none of these feels right, look elsewhere. Never be bamboozled into buying a suit that does not feel comfortable. If in doubt ask to be measured – across the chest, waist, hips, sleeve and trouser length. Never compromise on comfort (or, as far as economically possible, on quality) but do be prepared to take advice on trying a different style from the one you have always worn. A double-breasted suit for example may come as a pleasant surprise and a man who has hitherto favoured the lightweight Continental style and the man who has always dressed in the genuinely old, or the traditionally reworked may find himself seduced by the relaxed elegance of the Italian influence.

SEPARATES AS ALTERNATIVES

If you feel uncomfortable in a suit and are not required to wear one in the course of work, consider instead the 'semi-formality' of the classic jacket and trousers. Keep to 'city' colours – dark or mid-grey, navy blue and black. Match plain flannel trousers (not the harsh public-school kind! Flannel is now much softer, smoother and infinitely more comfortable) or wool with the best quality jacket you can find such as a quality blazer in finest wool. As you are likely to change trousers with separates more often than jackets, it is worth indulging in a luxury jacket which will 'lift' the whole outfit.

THE SECONDHAND SUIT

Separates are good investments for the older man on a budget but the young can find excellent suit bargains in secondhand shops. In the past few years, secondhand shops for men have improved and flourished. Many now offer designer suits at a fraction of their original price and this is an excellent way to indulge a desire for the latest fashion. London and big city shops lead the trend and it is here that the young man will need to look if he wants to find a secondhand Jean Paul Gaultier, but country shops can offer excellent bargains in separates (fine tweed jackets, blazers, plain trousers, coats) which also translate to city wear.

The secret is to go back frequently as good secondhand clothes at low prices don't usually hang around but don't purchase in too much of a hurry. Take time to examine the suit for missing buttons, a torn lining or loose threads and never buy anything which does not look clean. Once again, cut, cloth and comfort are important. A good classic shape in a quality material like pure wool is a bargain – but only if it fits properly and feels comfortable. Don't be seduced by label alone and resist Secondhand Horrors like the following:

- Suits that are 'stiff' (too much man-made fibre).

- Suits that are overtly 'fashionable' with shoulder pads a mile wide, with flared or skin-tight trousers, or with loose jackets which are so 'unstructured' they have no shape at all.

- Suits in 'unusual' patterns or colours (wide stripes, checks, shiny greys and light blues).

- 'Shag'-pile suits or jackets made from heavy-textured materials that will always look out of place in town.

All the above will have been someone else's mistake (which may be why they ended up in a secondhand shop). It takes real style to find a secondhand garment you can turn to good use and requires a great deal of effort. However, discovering the one true bargain can make it all worthwhile.

CHECKING THE DETAILS

Tailored, ready-made, new or secondhand, the details of pockets, vents, lapels, buttons and texture are all important. Shape, colour and pattern are part of the essential background to which these details give the finishing touch.

SHAPE. The shape of a suit is dictated by its cut which varies from the more traditional waisted, close-fitting shape to the large, loose form of recent fashion. The shape of the traditional Savile Row suit has changed little since the Thirties. It is still a single-breasted jacket with straight 'constructed' (semi-padded) shoulder line, slightly waisted and worn with straight trousers (no turn-ups) held up at the waist with a narrow belt or braces. The Continental suit is a slimmer version of the Savile Row classic. The lapels are usually narrower and the shoulders quite square. Double-breasted suits used to be like military greatcoats in that they

PUTTING IT ALL TOGETHER – THE QUIET
SHIRT WITH THE CONVENTIONAL TIE,
THE SMOOTH JACKET WITH JUST A HINT
OF CARELESSNESS IN THE POCKET
HANDKERCHIEF, THE CASHMERE COAT
CASUALLY HELD IN RESERVE. THIS IS THE
PERFECT OUTFIT FOR IMPRESSING THE
FUTURE MOTHER-IN-LAW ESPECIALLY IF
NOT TAKEN TOO SERIOUSLY.

had eight buttons and fastened solidly across the chest. The
more usual style nowadays has six buttons (the top two do not
fasten) or four buttons, worn with straight or turn-up trousers.

Your shape is equally important. The short man
should choose slim, tapered trousers with no turn-ups and
avoid anything voluminous. Jackets which are slightly built
up at the shoulders help increase the width and a square-cut
shape emphasises the leg in trousers. Avoid anything tight if
weight is a problem and keep the line simple. Double-breasted
suits can be 'slimming' but not for those on the short side as
they emphasise a 'square' look.

COLOUR, PATTERN AND TEXTURE. The darker the colour of a suit, the more 'serious' it looks. Dark suits always look best for formal occasions such as weddings and create a more sophisticated impression for business.

Some London City institutions like the Stock Exchange, still do not countenance anything they consider too frivolous, 'such as green', but the variations are now much wider than the traditional dark blue pinstripe. Houndstooth or bird's-eye dots and herringbone patterns are now acceptable and the chalk-stripe suit is ubiquitous. Plain blue, as already noted, can mark and shine quickly. Mid-grey, with a wide-ish chalk-stripe (not too wide for the short and fat) is practical because the stripe draws the eye and detracts from slight marks. But nothing can beat the traditional dark blue pinstripe for classic city stylishness. Single- or double-breasted, three-piece or two-piece suit, it provides the perfect 'business' background for the man who wishes to be taken seriously.

"Nicholas Ridley has style – an upper-class physical elegance

combined with a good mind and the swagger of the cavalryman.

Michael Heseltine has bags of it, so has Nicholas Soames,

though Geoffrey Howe has none. Alan Clark also has it. He

was once asked if he was in favour of poll tax and replied that of

course he was as he lived in a house with 143 rooms."
JULIAN CRITCHLEY, MP

City suits (and those worn for any formal occasion) are always smooth textured. Heavy textures are for country wear and even then, should be treated with care as they can add to the impression of 'girth'.

VENTS. Vents give 'movement' to a jacket. Whether you have one, two or none is mostly a question of personal preference. Single vents used to be favoured by Americans on their larger, more loosely structured suits and are useful

It's the details that really count.
A sharp cuff teamed with a well-
lined sleeve (above) and a simple
dot and pin-stripe (below). Style
lies in simplicity rather than
matching sets of things.

because they make it easier to put hands in pockets. They should always hang straight. If the 'vent pulls open at the back when the jacket is buttoned, the jacket needs more room at the waist. Double vents are more traditionally 'English' and more practical for anyone who spends a lot of time sitting down as the flap can be tucked beneath the buttocks and it doesn't crease so readily as a single vent. Continental suits (including many designer suits) usually have no vents at all. Check that the back of the jacket hangs straight and doesn't crease in a ridge when you sit down.

BUTTONS. A good suit does not need buttons if it is properly balanced. If a jacket hangs properly from the shoulders, the front will naturally fall in line without fastening. It is hard to put to the test as most suits do have buttons. But the position at which they are sewn to the material can be crucial. When fastened, buttons should never cause material to crinkle, crease or 'pull'. Most single-breasted suits have two or three buttons, of which, only the middle or top button is fastened. However, the rule must depend ultimately on individual preference as how you button your jacket is not so much a matter of style as of comfort.

Sleeve buttons are a test of quality on a garment. Those which unfasten are much more stylish (and practical) than those which do not. As the author of *The English Gentleman* cheerfully notes: 'The criterion of a gentleman's suit is that it should fit well round the shoulders and that the cuff buttons should undo so that he can turn them back when he is washing his hands.'

Always test that buttons are firmly hand sewn to jackets and look for the 'cross stitch' on button holes which usually denotes that these have also been finished by hand.

LAPEL SIZE. Lapel size usually varies in proportion with the shape of the suit. Slim-fitting narrow-waisted single-breasted suits, for example, usually carry narrower lapels than a more 'roomy' double-breasted suit. The two main kinds of lapels are the 'notched' and the 'peaked' and the real difference between them is that the former invariably appear on single-breasted jackets while the peaked variety are more common on double-breasted suits (though they are also used for formal dinner jackets, perhaps because they traditionally carry a button hole on each lapel). The width of the lapel can quickly date a suit. This is most obvious on dinner jackets as men renew them so infrequently but even on suits kept for a shorter period of time a subtle change in lapel width can outmode a suit and date its wearer as obviously as the wrong shape of tie.

POCKETS. Once again, the number of pockets you have in your suits is really a matter of personal preference. Too many unbalance the suit and can add to an impression of width. The usual style is one pocket on each hip with a smaller breast pocket on the top left-hand side. Good details to watch for are 'jetted' and 'flapped' pockets on which the flap fits neatly inside or outside the line of the pocket and a 'two-way' inside pocket which means that you can tuck the top of your wallet into a fold in the lining to help prevent it sliding out. Some inside jacket pockets have small button flaps for the same purpose. Pockets should be deep enough to fit the hand and properly lined.

JACKET LININGS. Sad to say, most ready-made suits use synthetic material for lining. The more traditional silk twill is generally only found in tailor-made or made-to-order suits.

'Contrast' silk linings can certainly add style to a suit but it is easy to descend from the sublime to the ridiculous. Rich colours (dark blue, burgundy, paisley patterns) can work well to add informality to a dark suit but they should not be too 'eye-catching', if only for practical reasons, as the more dramatic the jacket lining, the harder it is to match shirt and tie without looking as if you've overdone it. City suits look best with plain linings (at their most formal with sleeves traditionally lined in striped cotton to match the inside back of the waistcoat and trousers). The result need not be boring if you select a slightly more unusual shade like pale oyster grey or raspberry.

Less formal suits or jackets in fine tweed often have contrasting cotton linings – a more Continental custom which works with sweaters and Viyella shirts better than with formal city shirts.

WAISTCOATS. Three-piece suits have returned to fashion since a decline dating back to the rigours of clothes rationing after the Second World War. Waistcoats, once a symbol of tailor-made, are now available off-the-peg in a

BOTH WAISTCOATS ARE
STYLISH VARIATIONS ON THE MORE
TRADITIONAL 'THREE-PIECE' AND
COMBINE PRACTICAL COMFORT
WITH EYE-CATCHING
INTEREST.

variety of colours and fabrics. The safest way to wear these is with other separates. However, the addition of some kind of waistcoat to a two-piece suit can transform the complete outfit. For more sober business occasions, choose dark colours but experiment with different materials – a wool or cashmere button-through slipover for example, worn with top button left open. Silk always looks 'dressy', flannel is more sporty but comes in wonderful 'hunting colours' such as red and yellow

A RATHER BRACING WAY TO START THE
DAY IS THE SLAP IN THE FACE
TECHNIQUE.

which give a terrific lift to plain casual jackets and trousers.

The traditional tailored waistcoat is one of the most difficult garments to cut and fit, so when done well it is a work of art. The front should never pouch or bag and the waistcoat should fit neatly into the waist. Waistcoats are warm, and useful places for storing accessories like pens, pocket watches and Albert chains. They also keep the front of the suit looking 'tidy' especially for those who remove their jackets to work in shirt sleeves. Most of all, the more gaudy variety are *fun* and an instant way to achieve a more flamboyant style. It takes nerve to flaunt yourself in watered silk or satin and like bow ties, the jaunty waistcoat gives an impression of artful frivolity. This makes them ideal for semi-formal weddings or cutting a dash at dinner parties and for daywear in media, marketing and publishing work.

PERSONAL CARE

No clothing, however elegant, can compensate for sloppy posture or a neglected appearance evident in a poor shave, a dirty complexion, scruffy hairstyle or dirty fingernails.

STRAIGHT BACK AND SIDES. A well-cut suit can hide a multitude of sins but the shape of the man inside is very important. Posture can transform appearance and even the stout man looks more elegant if he carries himself well. Avoid the 'military bearing' if it means throwing the chest out and the shoulders back. Instead, stretch the body up from the waist (as in riding) and allow the shoulders to relax.

FACIAL FEATURES. Cleanliness is primordial in acquiring style. Sweat and oil glands are most active from mid-teens to thirties but deep cleansing helps control the oil supply. Use soap and warm water, or a medicated cleansing bar for problem skin. Splash with plenty of warm water and finish off with cold. Help keep shirt collars clean by washing the neck daily with soap and water or wipe down with a pad of damp cotton wool soaked in pore-refining lotion (purchased from the toiletries department of department stores and chemists) – a particularly effective way of cleansing necks prone to spots and rashes.

Treat oily face patches with medicated lotions, paying particular attention to nose, chin, forehead but don't overdo it or skin will get dry and irritated.

If skin is very sensitive and dry, try softening up with a moisturiser five minutes before shaving. Choose from a range designed for men as these are usually less greasy. Avoid alcohol-based lotions.

Watch the diet. Too much drink, stress and smoking depletes vitamin supply. Eat plenty of fresh vegetables and fruit and cleanse a clogged system by drinking lots of spring water. Exercise helps boost circulation but always shower after a work-out to cleanse and tone skin.

Try a face and body scrub. Face scrubs are good weekly treatments. Use body and hair shampoos for after-sports cleansing. Treat yourself to the occasional facial. Many barbers now extend the hot towel routine to include aromatherapy treatments which are not only deep cleansing but very relaxing.

SHAVING NOTES. Two out of three British men prefer to wet shave with a blade but once you practise this method it's harder to get a close dry shave which is more practical for the frequent traveller. Choose a blade that's sharp along its entire length. How long it will continue to give a close shave depends on the texture of stubble but rinsing the blade well after each use and keeping it scrupulously clean will definitely help prolong its life.

Preparation – all important for a good wet shave. Wash face with warm water (too hot will cause the skin to swell). Rinse well before applying foam or cream and work into face to help soften up bristles before shaving. Start at the hair junction by the ear and shave downwards. Shave under chin from front to back, stretching the neck up (helps depress the Adam's apple). Shave upper lip last – these are toughest hairs so need more time to soften up – with short, downward strokes. For a closer cut, shave cheeks again in opposite (upward) direction, against growth of beard.

Aftercare – rinse face and razor. Splashing with cold water helps close pores. Apply aftershave with discrimination. Too much will not only offend fellow travellers, but high alcohol content can 'burn' and dry sensitive skin.

Dry shaving: because the shaving edge of electrics doesn't get so close to the skin, whiskers need to be encouraged to stand out more. A pre-electric shave lotion or some other form of astringent will help this. It will also remove some of the dirt and oils on skin and lubricate the face to prevent razor drag.

Sore points such as razor bumps (caused when newly shaved hair gets trapped under surface of the skin) and rash can both be helped by a good aftershave balm. These contain moisturisers to soothe and soften small cuts and work as a frag-rant disinfectant. Smoothed into skin after shaving, they are kinder to the complexion than heavily perfumed aftershaves.

HAIRCARE. A good cut is essential. It can make hair look thicker and takes years off age so look first for a good barber or hairdresser. Haircare is made easier with good conditioning shampoos for men that are less heavily scented than the female variety. Frequent washing does not encourage hair loss and lank, greasy hair looks far worse on a thinning head than short, clean hair.

Dandruff is a scalp condition aggravated by stress. Severe cases may be a type of psoriasis and need medical attention. Minor problems can be solved with a treatment shampoo though prolonged use of some of these can do more harm than good as they contain a detergent which stimulates the sebaceous glands. Jojoba oil is good for scalp conditions when regularly massaged into the head but poor diet can also cause dandruff (and encourage hair loss) so check up on vitamin and mineral intake.

Most lotions and potions 'guaranteed' to stimulate regrowth are, so far, just optimism. Better to take care of what's already there than to hope for resurrection.

Colour restorers are metallic-based liquids that build up dark colour through the hair and don't actually 'restore' anything. Hair colouring is a new concept for men but 'comb-through' colourants provide a subtle introduction. Bleaches and permanent tints need constant retouching and always look unnatural. Perming can add body to hair and lasts for about three months. Once curled, hair has to grow to get back to its natural condition. Hair straightening is complicated, hardly worth the effort and only to be tried by a really good and confident hairdresser.

HANDCARE. Hands have always been an indication of a gentleman and used to be a sign of class and occupation. Nowadays they are more an indication of character as the man who cares about his hands cares about his whole appearance and about other people. Women notice hands almost as much as face and figure, and a grubby 'paw' can be very disturbing. Keep fingernails cut short and as clean as possible. If you need help, get a professional manicure. Most big city department stores offer a manicure service for men and so do some hairdressers and barbers. Clean and buff nails regularly. Never varnish.

CHAPTER THREE

THE ENGLISHMAN AT LEISURE

"The BBC once said I resembled a broken–down English country house. I don't know if they were being complimentary but I do think an Englishman's style is different from other people's – rather like gardens. The French, for example, are much more formal."

SIR NICHOLAS HENDERSON,
former ambassador to Washington and Paris

'Off duty' casual clothing allows for more opportunity to experiment with colour, material and the addition of the personal touch than city working dress. Fewer rules should make for more fluidity but, as with sex, rigid preconception can swiftly spoil the pleasure.

First, there are those who are simply lazy. If they are not required to make the effort, they don't. Then there are those who confuse style with 'dressing up' and think the subject out of context in the countryside. Finally, there are those who simply revert to another kind of uniform.

Certain clothes, like Barbours, Burberrys and Huskies have become symbols of something more than mere comfort. They are now status clothing which have received universal acceptance as the 'correct' dress for wear in the English countryside.

Of course, there is nothing wrong with the clothes themselves, but the self-imposed regimentation does the Englishman a disservice, as his traditional casual clothing is genuinely unique.

In purist form, it is based on a practical *mélange* of well-worn, much loved hand-me-downs or school clothing, punctuated with the occasional horrendous sweater knitted by Granny, nanny or some other old retainer. Whether he lives in a castle or a cottage, the Englishman has a fine sense of history and his clothes are often part of his past. Many a divorce has been caused by the insensitivity of a wife who simply could not appreciate that though it has holes in the elbows and smells like a damp sheep, a much-loved pullover is more indispensable than she is.

This kind of 'matured' clothing is one style which is useless to try to imitate. It really is a matter of being born to the cloth and of appreciating, in the words of Rupert Brooke, 'the smell of old clothes'.

For that reason alone, not everyone would *want* to try to emulate it. Visitors to Britain are often appalled by the off-duty dishevelment of colleagues who turn from models of working refinement during the week into walking jumble collections at the weekend. Most visitors are also totally unprepared for the mud-wallowing, marrow-freezing nature of English countryside activities.

The more traditional Englishman spends his country

weekends getting back to his roots. This is true in the metaphorical sense in that the clothing he adopts for working wear often has its origins in country sporting clothes – the vents in a suit jacket, for example, are derived from the split riding coat. But it is also literally so, and vividly reflected in the Englishman's passion for digging.

Everyone knows how deeply the English are devoted to gardens. Their lawns are the envy of the world and so are their roses. Much unexpected emotion and energy goes into planting and pruning and very little time is actually spent simply 'admiring'. No matter how large or small his estate, the Englishman will spend at least part of his weekend digging it and whether he is digging for foxes or for parsnips, he will do it in old clothes.

This then, is deemed the first prerequisite for traditional country style. Clothes must look tried, tested and most of all, comfortable. Anything that looks new immediately seems suspect. The only way a town-bred man can hope to compensate for turning up in a smart new coat or jacket is to stun his critics with a demonstration of an encyclopaedic knowledge of greenfly or beagling.

This rule of 'old' applies particularly to Barbours, Huskies and Puffas, which in recent years have become so universally popular. Waxed jackets and green wellington boots should never look new. It is more a question of looking at ease than of snobbery, but the Englishman is sometimes blinded to the fact that a man can look just as 'comfortable' in a clean sweater of unusual colour and interesting design as in an old navy blue garment that the dog has slept on.

His assumption that casual clothes are by definition 'ancient' deprives him of the opportunity to indulge his sense of adventure. With a modicum of effort, he can easily put together a country collection that will still be comfortable but whose eccentricity relies more on inspiration than mere habit.

MATERIALS

The material of clothes becomes a critical point in country wear. Natural fibres are much more at home here than synthetics. They are warmer, more comfortable and age well. When buying, it pays to plan around the following fibres:

PURE WOOL works for almost any type of clothing.

Country colours blend with the
background so that they do not
startle the wild-life but
experiment with interesting
weaves and textures and
unexpected colour combinations.

Lightweight flannel and wool gaberdine works well for casual trousers, and knitwear is still surprisngly inexpensive and good value for money.

TWEED now comes in a variety of thicknesses and patterns. The heavy, traditional types in Glen checks, Donegal speckle and Harris fleck can be tough, almost thornproof, reflecting the working life of the areas where the material was originally woven. Softer tweeds with a more Continental influence translate well from country to town wear and look just as much 'in place' worn with a shirt as with a sweater.

CASHMERE is the top range in knitted luxury. It is graded by thickness (ply) and the price varies accordingly. In some cases, it may be better to buy a thick lambswool or shetland for country wear than a very fine cashmere but there is nothing to beat a fine quality four-ply cashmere sweater in a classic ribbed style with a round or V-neck. All knitwear needs some care in handling and washing if it is to keep its shape and attention should be paid to the instructions on the label. In general, a good cashmere pullover does not need too much special attention as the fibres are so fine and soft that they are naturally resilient.

COTTON is one of the most versatile natural materials and also the cheapest. It works for almost everything in a variety of textures, including velvet, corduroy, denim and shirting. Cotton can be cool but also warm when used as lining material for waterproof jackets for raincoats. Cotton knits make good summer items for casual city wear but always look for good quality. 'Cheap' corduroy for example soon wears and like cheap velvet, goes 'bald' and patchy.

FORMAL COUNTRY WEAR

COATS. Country coats must first fit the criteria of being warm and waterproof. Waxed coats are both. They are also very practical as they contain lots of useful pockets and are light and comfortable to wear. The traditional green waxed jackets only protect the body as far as the knees. The full-length waxed coat is the best protection for really rough weather but it does not translate as well to town wear.

A good tweed coat in traditional houndstooth or herringbone, works well for both country and town wear and is warm and practical, though not entirely rainproof. The 'Loden' is also a good town and country coat. In traditional green, the original comes from the Austrian Tyrol where it takes its name from the 'Loderer' or wool weaver. The special method of matting the cloth to give it 'stritch' results in a light but very warm coat which is also showerproof. The cut of the coat usually incorporates an unstitched section to the armholes which gives extra room and movement, ideal for wearing the coat over jackets or heavy textured pullovers.

Loden coats have a European character which almost makes them an international badge. In the past they have appeared in only the most 'travelled' English wardrobe but are now gaining popularity as a useful coat for the town-based businessman who only has time to visit the country rather than live in it.

Raincoats are not usually warm enough for the cold of the British countryside unless they have a good thick detachable lining. The stone-coloured trenchcoat looks out of place against a background of green fields so choose instead a green or slate-blue colour. Rubberised raincoats cut in the shape of long riding coats are good waterproof garments for wear over warm sweaters but keep to traditional styling and avoid anything with too much fashion detail.

COUNTRY SUITS AND JACKETS. Tweed suits are an excellent example of the 'old' principle. Many are antiquated and often inherited, made in a coarse material that lasts through several lifetimes. The new 'Continental' tweeds are softer and more subtly coloured and do just as well for Sunday drinks and church.

Increasingly, semi-formal separates have come to replace the country suit. Jackets in plain, patterned, smooth or more coarsely textured wools provide an excellent background for creating a 'mixed and matched' style using scarves, wool polo shirts and different coloured knitwear. If the jacket has more than one colour in it, choose accessories that pick up a predominant colour and don't be afraid to contrast checks with spots or stripes.

COUNTRY SUITS AND JACKETS PUT
COMFORT FIRST. POUCHY JACKETS WITH
PLENTY OF POCKET ROOM, WARM CORD
TROUSERS WITH GOOD, DEEP POCKETS.
GLOVES ALSO SERVE A WARMING
PURPOSE.

Sheepskin jackets became fashionable with the MGB sportscar. Every young man called Nigel hurtling off to a point-to-point shrouded himself in a sheepskin and they are still popular at Game Fairs and Agricultural Shows. They are warm and hardwearing but all too often are 'over-designed' with unnecessary additions, so look for a style which is plain and unadorned.

COUNTRY TROUSERS. Tweed jackets work with almost any material from denim jeans to corduroy. The thicker the texture of the material, the more 'countrified' it is. Heavy textured tweeds, thick flannel, wide-ribbed cords, cavalry twill, all have an 'earthy' look which makes the

LEFT. NEUTRAL TWIN-SET IS THE TOP OF
THE CLASSIC CREAM. ABOVE, HOW TO
CHECK OUT THE FAIRWAY.

material more at home in the country than the town. The really heavy textured tweeds are particularly 'regional'; they always look better on the grouse moors of Scotland than in, say, the gentler climate of the Cotswolds.

Country trousers should be warm and loose fitting with the accent on comfort and plenty of room for movement.

COUNTRY SHIRTS. Country shirts are usually made in 'warmer' material such as Viyella and are traditionally patterned in Tattersall checks. The purists have them made in Jermyn Street, but they can also be purchased ready-made from shops and department stores.

The traditional Englishman still tends to dress for dinner on Saturday nights in the country. His wife will wear an ancient velvet skirt with frilly blouse and he will dress in a suit (or perhaps a blazer and dark trousers) and a cotton shirt.

Ordinary cotton shirts or polo styles look infinitely better under classic V-neck sweaters than round-neck T-shirts.

COUNTRY KNITWEAR. Country knits should be warm and reasonably hard wearing. Heavily ribbed or cabled design adds to the 'chunkiness' of the texture. Traditional styled arrans and guernseys usually come in blues, greens and cream but this is the opportunity to experiment with earthy colours of brown mixed with heather blues, pinks, mauves and a wide variety of soft shades. Look for traditional patterns in Fair-Isles or fisherman's knits in preference to solid, bright colours as these match more successfully with the popular greens, blues and browns of country jackets.

FOOTWEAR. Country shoes must be practical. A pair of wellington boots are essential for any weekend activity which involves patrolling the 'estate' or even the smallest garden. Good lace-up leather brogues are best for walking but they must be comfortable and large enough to wear with thick

GOOD, RICH EARTHY COLOURS
ARE ALWAYS RELIABLE

THERE'S ALWAYS A WARM WELLIE IN
THE HILLSIDES, AND A MORE CLASSIC
VERSION OF THE PERENNIAL DUFFLE
COAT.

socks. Desert boots and suede shoes are not practical country wear, nor are plimsolls as they absorb water, don't protect the ankles and are difficult to clean.

COUNTRY TIES AND CRAVATS. The 'country' tie worn with the Viyella check shirt usually sprouts an amazing collection of wildlife (pheasants or wild duck) and is generally made of wool. A tie is a sign of formality so it can be more comfortable to replace it with a cravat or silk scarf.

Cravats suffer from a rather 'county' image and are still sometimes associated with dark blue blazers and the gin-and-tonic set. But they make practical casual wear as they are easy to tie (like a scarf), comfortable and they provide an excellent weekend alternative to the more restricting necktie. Tweed jackets, blazers (try striped cotton as a change to dark blue for summer) make a good background for cravats.

Dots and paisley are traditional but flowers and geometric designs add to the frivolity associated with the history of cravats. Beau Brummell was famous for his and had extraordinary names for some of them such as The Cascade, The Horsey and The Sentimental. Later, he went in for heavily starched varieties which were reportedly responsible for dismembering ears and dislocating necks.

Brummell is said to have started the fashion for cravats because he needed to hide his swollen neck glands which may also be worth consideration if you suddenly find yourself with mumps.

HATS. Country hats should be chosen for warmth and water-resistance more than fashion. The flat cap is the most popular country headwear but it flatters few men as it really only suits a large, square face. Invariably styled in tweed (to match the tweed suit), it is most comfortable if worn low on the forehead, not skiing down the back of the head.

NOTES FOR THE WEEKEND GUEST

An invitation to a country home contains a variety of hidden pitfalls. First, find out how your host spends his weekend – it may change your mind about accepting the invitation. Dress accordingly for any sporting activities (*see Chapter 4*) but in any case, take warm clothing and practical footwear. (If you arrive in boots don't forget a change of shoes for the house.) Pack warm pyjamas and a really thick wool dressing gown as many English country houses lack effective central heating and *en suite* bathrooms.

Thermal underwear, thick woollen socks, warm gloves, woollen scarf are all useful extras for winter weekends – often for summer too! To these add your own brand of soap, hand towel and hairdryer (you will never find one provided and it could be embarrassing to have to borrow), clean money (if there are likely to be staff who will need to be tipped) and an original present for your hostess – not chocolates!

NOTES FOR THE WEEKEND GUEST
CONTINUED: KEEP THE HOSTESS
AMUSED. WEAR CLOTHES THAT FIT THE
OCCASION – NOTHING TOO NEW FOR
THE COUNTRY.

ANOTHER ALTERNATIVE CASUAL IS THE
WEEKEND WOMAN WORN DRAPED
AROUND THE SHOULDERS. THE LOOSE,
COTTON JACKET MAKES EXCELLENT
SUMMER WEAR.

Not everyone loves the country. There is a growing breed of young Englishmen who spend their entire lives in cities. They feed from supermarkets, confine their knowledge of botany to a few flower stalls and go out to graze in the city boutiques.

The City Dude is a transatlantic character and much of his style has devolved from the influence of the United States. He has the body for T-shirts and jeans and is not afraid to wear colour. He is also the man who prefers walking in city parks to hoofing it through some God-forsaken moorland, who enjoys being within reach of theatre, opera and art galleries and relishes the 'closed-for-lunch' feel of capital cities at the weekend. He simply does not experience the masochistic compulsion to head to the fields and breathe lungfuls of dung-perfumed air, especially if he has been spared the experience of the British public school.

These are the new type of Englishmen – young, fit, built in American Bruce Weber style. They pump iron in gyms to keep in shape, watch their diets and, unlike their country cousins, have real muscle to show for it.

They also dress extremely well in a transatlantic fashion which still holds to the basic British principle of comfort first. But it is their sense of colour that really excels in contrast to the browns, blues and greens of their country cousins.

Each can learn from the other as English country gentleman and contemporary city man both have the same end in mind, to feel confident and at ease in their clothes. The major difference lies in the fact that the city man considers clothes more carefully and is prepared to invest in the new and experimental.

Current British fashion owes a lot to American, Japanese and Continental design and the dedicated follower works hard at his research. He probably takes advice from magazines and television programmes, adapts his style from films and photographs, but to avoid mistakes in shopping around he needs a system.

The French have a habit worth imitating. They invest in the best for basics, then each year study the fashion trends and buy one or two garments which really reflect the current mood. It's a play-off of old and new, a mixture of straightforward taste and tradition and it makes them among the most economical and the most fashionably dressed in the world.

Even the sharpest of Style Counsellors can look uniform. Too much 'loose, unstructured clothing' can leave a man looking like a refugee from a ready-to-wear catwalk. *Personal* style still counts but once again, before spraying on the individual touch, the basics must be right. 'Invest in the best' is still a good motto.

DENIM. Jeans are one of the few items of clothing which really do suit most shapes and most age groups.

The best denim is soft but strong and goes on for ever. Good jeans are distinguished by the material – sixteen-ounce cotton – and by the quality of top-stitching. Zip and stud flies are both popular and equally dangerous if no underwear is worn. Rustproof rivets help strengthen the pockets on some makes but, as with a good suit, the most important feature is cut and comfort. Well-cut jeans fit without pinching and do not require a great deal of post-purchase shrinking.

Denim jeans and jackets now come in a wide variety of styles and pre-conditioning. They may be bleached, distressed, stonewashed, moonwashed, acidwashed and snowwashed. They may also be cut second-skin tight or baggy, in traditional blue, black, khaki or stone. They can change 'appearance' from drop-dead casual to off-duty chic and suit any mood from brooding artiness (designer stubble and a luxurious black cashmere polo shirt) to academic ease (white shirt, tweed jacket or blazer).

Jeans are one of the few really international garments that translate across all cultures and are now worn or coveted in almost every country in the world.

Contrary to popular belief, jeans were not invented

REAL STYLE IS SIMPLE. THE CONFIDENT
USE OF CLOTHES TO PROJECT YOUR
PERSONALITY. COOL, RELAXED, YOU
JUST KNOW THIS MAN WASHES HIS
UNDERPANTS.

in the USA but in the Italian city of Genoa in the nineteenth century – which is where the word 'jean' originates. The garments were first worn by Genoese sailors. 'Denim' is a corruption of 'de Nîmes' referring to the French town where durable cotton was woven.

Claude Levi-Strauss was a German Jewish immigrant who owned a trading store in San Francisco during the Californian gold rush. In 1873, he registered the patent for a tough kind of trouser made out of a fabric he had imported from Europe and the Levi was born.

Jeans were worn almost exclusively by miners and cowboys until the 1950s when Marlon Brando and James Dean made them the uniform of the young. The US government ensured their success by having jeans banned from high schools. But in the 1980s, disaster struck the jean industry when the garments became unfashionable. Levi cut staff by over fifteen thousand, reverted to private ownership and moved back to its roots in the same San Francisco site originally owned by Claude Levi-Strauss. Thus Levis became a 'traditional' garment and one with a heritage, but it was advertising and 'image' models like Nick Kamen who helped establish 501s as the jeans with style.

Versatility has ensured the survival of jeans, but they also fulfil the criterion of any good item of clothing: they are hardwearing and practical and they have certainly earned themselves a dominant place in the history of clothes in the twentieth century.

CASUAL JACKETS. City jackets should have social credibility and the best are the suedes and leathers that are too refined to work in the country. Cut must be good and the leather really soft. Look for simple lines and avoid anything fringed or with too much detail. Classic shapes are the blouson or the straight leather jacket which falls to mid-hip. But casual cotton 'blazer' styles also work well in summer with T-shirts and white cotton 'chino' trousers. Summer jackets are an excellent way of mixing and matching colour inexpensively and trying out new styles that can later be translated to more formal – and more costly – suits.

SWEATERS. For many, this is the colour cue. Most Englishmen are naturally wary of bright colours but casual city wear and untraditional sports clothes give excellent opportunities for breaking out of the 'service' blues and greens.

Lambswool is always a good buy. Shapes proliferate but the basics are crew-neck, V-neck, turtle-neck and polo-neck. Colours now vary from bright to pale pastels.

Sweaters can provide a fashionable twist to casual wear. Fair-Isles for example, have coasted in and out of fashion in the Eighties, promoted by films and TV serials reflecting the 1920s when they were first made popular as golf clothing by Edward Prince of Wales. 'Slipovers' with ribbed neck and waist and knitted waistcoats in 1930s style have also moved in and out of the fashion headlines. Many of the 'designer' styles can be imitated through less expensive outlets and it is worth 'trying out' a style before spending too much, as sweaters can alter the shape of the body's outline.

SWEATER NOTES

1 Bulky handmade sweaters make the wearer look 'heavy'. V-necks with set-in sleeves in a lightweight wool make the torso look longer and slimmer.

2 Heavy men should avoid sweaters and shirts with bright horizontal stripes. But these are ideal for those on the thin side. Horizontal stripes are also useful for the very tall as they 'cut' the line of the body and help minimise height. Vertical stripes and patterns help elongate the body.

3 Sweaters with padded shoulders look best on those whose hips are the same width, or wider than the shoulders. They make a wide-shouldered man look too broad. Boat necks (most popular in cotton for summer wear as a shirt doesn't sit comfortably under them) also add width to the shoulders. The very broadchested are better off with raglan sleeves which help reduce shoulder width. Raglans also help 'correct' the look of sloping shoulders. Raglan sleeves give an illusion of length to short arms and horizontal stripes help disguise a humped back. Showing shirt cuffs beneath a sweater 'shortens' the arm, so do horizontal stripes on the sleeves.

4 Crew-necks, polo-necks and turtle-necks help hide an obtrusive Adam's apple or a long neck, while V-neck sweaters add length to a 'bull' neck.

COLOUR

'Colour counselling' need not inhibit the style conscious or the man who instinctively knows what he likes but beware regimentation into anything too defined. Few men have good colour sense (and many are genuinely 'colour-blind') so on this occasion it could help to take a woman along for a second opinion as your own favourite colours may not necessarily be those which suit you best.

Choose colour by holding the garment across the shoulder against the neck, not up in front of the face. Does it diminish the shadows round the jawline and eyes, make the heart lift and the years fall away? If so, buy it immediately. Always buy colours that invite compliments from others – they get to see the whole effect and are probably less prejudiced in their opinion than you are.

TROUSERS

Cotton is a favourite fabric for the casual city trouser – in corduroy, denim or mixed with linen. These work through most seasons but on the rare days the sun shines warm in Britain, the experience hits the population with collective lunacy.

The truly traditional Englishman takes no notice. He will continue to wear his city suit in a tropical heatwave and his blazer to Henley in the pouring rain. But the young man-about-town goes berserk and appears on the city streets in 'holiday' shorts.

It is hard to look smart in shorts, even for an army officer. In civilian life a man can look athletic, sexy or like a boy scout but he rarely looks stylish. It is something to do with the British figure. Californians and Australians have the instant advantage of being tanned but the average Englishman's legs hang below shorts like bits of white string.

At such times as the occasional heatwave, the average Englishman's sense of appropriateness seems to desert him completely. If you must wear shorts in town, choose the longer, more tailored kind in linen or cotton. Team them with an equally casual top – T-shirt, short-sleeved shirt, cotton pullover or a polo shirt.

One of the best inventions in contemporary menswear, the polo shirt combines elegance and ease for all

THE CLASSIC POLO SHIRT – AT EASE IN
MOST CASUAL SITUATIONS, IT ALSO
ALLOWS FOR EXPERIMENT WITH NEW
COLOUR COMBINATIONS WITHIN A
CLASSIC FRAMEWORK.

seasons. In long- or short-sleeved version, with a variety of collar styles, the best are manufactured in 'mercerised' cotton which gives a distinctive sheen to the fabric. Look for a collar opening that lies flat and is hand sewn, its inside edge finished with tape. Make sure the stripes match all round the garment, especially at the side seams and look for styles with 'graded' colours which are more subtle than those with distinctly contrasting stripes.

EXPERIMENT WITH CASUALS

Casual clothes, for whatever occasion, provide the best opportunity for making the most of inspiration. Use them to change mood, inject some fantasy into reality and express a variety of influences. Put together a series of contrasts – different fabrics, classics with high fashion or sporting clothes, experimental colour combinations – which all rely on inspiration rather than straight logic. Practice is the only way to learn but casuals provide the training ground on which to develop that confident touch of wit which characterises interesting style.

PRACTICE MAKES PERFECT AND
TIGHTENING UP ON THE DETAILS BRINGS
EVERYTHING INTO FOCUS.

CHAPTER FOUR

THE SPORTING ENGLISHMAN

"I wouldn't take my shirt off on the pitch. There's no need. New lighter materials keep you cool enough, though I would like to see more colour in cricket and the odd bit of styling. But I'm resistent to heavy use of logos and wouldn't like to see cricket clothes used like advertisement hoardings."

DAVID GOWER, cricketer

Sportswear has done much to revolutionise men's clothing in the last decade. Designers opened up the market for their clothes to a wider income bracket by producing 'sports' ranges which offered a less expensive way of wearing the 'label'.

Cheaper travel helped, giving the opportunity for more people to sample and enjoy 'new' sports abroad, such as mountain skiing and windsurfing.

Perhaps most significant of all was the rise of the cult of the healthy body. Body building, cleanliness and a new emphasis on masculinity replaced the scruffy 'femininity' of much of the Sixties and the 'liberalism' of the Seventies. Oiled muscularity drew reference from another kind of classic – that of the Greek athlete.

The disease AIDS not only made homosexuality a common talking point, it also encouraged an emphasis on clean living. The Yuppies also projected an image of 'work hard, play hard' that made good health a measure of success – once more, it was the survival of the fittest.

Sport has broken down many of the social barriers that remain in Britain. Once, football was for the industrial working classes, and, with the possible exception of cricket, everything else was for the better off. In Edwardian times, when British sport flourished (Great Britain won fifty-six gold medals in the 1908 Olympic Games), social distinctions were as defined in sport as in the outside world.

C.B. Fry typified the Edwardian gentleman who excelled at sport. He played cricket and captained England against Australia in 1902. He also played football to Cup Final level, boxed, golfed, was a good swimmer, a good shot, an excellent horseman and fisherman and could also throw the javelin. There is a story that at the inter-university sports in Oxford in 1892, he put down his cigar in the changing room and went out to break the world record for the long jump before returning to his smoke.

Characters like Fry were portrayed in the film 'Chariots of Fire' which showed the struggles of two men from very different backgrounds to succeed in athletics, and also emphasised the 'noble' aspect of sport. It seemed that 'style' in competition was not so much a question of clothing as of comportment.

Much of the clothing worn today for the 'tra-

ditional' country spectator sports has changed very little from
Edwardian times. Some of it has found wider popular appeal
as 'casual' clothing (hacking jackets, tweed coats and the polo
shirt), though not all – top hats are still worn to Ascot, though
they have not yet been taken up as fashion items by the young.

Certain sporting activities remain the prerogative of
the English country gentleman but the class barriers which
were once so strong have been eroded by the arrival of new
competitors from home and abroad.

The Traditional Sporting 'Uniform'

Traditionally, the sport of the English country gentleman has
always involved killing wildlife or the use of horses. Blood

sports take precedence over games early in life and indoctrination begins with useful little rhymes of a cautionary nature such as:

'Never, never let your gun,
pointed be at anyone . . .
All the pheasants ever bred
Will not make up for one man dead.'

FOX HUNTING. The sight of a hunt in full cry with riders decked out in black top hats and hunting pink has inspired many a fine print of English country life but not all Englishmen.

Doctor Johnson was one of those who found the sport unpalatable but it was Oscar Wilde who made himself the most famous opponent with his comment that fox hunting was 'the unspeakable in pursuit of the uneatable'.

Since fox hunting became invaded by the animal preservation league and celebrities from the Sixties, it has lost much of its John Bull appeal. Red and black frock coats worn with top hats, buckskin breeches and top boots disappeared around 1925. After that, the frock coat appeared in single-breasted style and full-skirted morning coats and swallowtails were also worn. The dedicated still wear black leather boots with a garter strap attached and the 'blue and buff' of the Beaufort Hunt is an elegy in antiquated elegance.

Nowadays, despite increasing costs, all sorts of people hunt, from doctors and dentists to publicans and postmen. Most wear stretch nylon breeches that do nothing to disguise a spreading rump and people increasingly 'ride out' in Huskies, old macs and a mixture of clothing. But nothing can beat the elegance of a traditional hunting jacket, set off by a white stock and breeches.

Hunting still holds attraction for the upwardly mobile as sitting on a horse gives an instant sense of superiority.

SHOOTING. 'Hunting is good exercise for a man of rank, but shooting is amusement equally lawful and proper for inferior persons,' stated Bishop Latimer in 1820.

Dress is extremely traditional and hardly changed from pre-First World War: tweed jackets (real, heavy tweed) with breeches or plus-fours, thick woollen shooting stockings, boots or sturdy full 'gillie' brogues and flat caps or

Prince Philip at the Windsor Horse
Show, a perfect portrait of the
Sporting Englishman.

appropriately 'helmet' shapes with ear flaps tied on top. However, Barbours have also made their way on to the moors and into the woodlands, as have Huskies, Hunters and green corduroy trousers.

Shooting is a serious business and, like war, mostly left to men. Therefore, although there is pressure to look smart, it is definitely not a fashion event and the most important thing is to look 'appropriate' and fit in.

Spectator Style

The same criterion applies to all clothing worn by spectators of country sports from horse trials to point-to-points. As with all country wear, nothing should appear startlingly 'new' and, like the young Heathcliffe, men should always look as rugged and craggy as possible.

> *Let other people play at other things,*
> *the king of games is still the game of kings.*

(inscribed on a stone tablet near a polo ground in Gilgit, Pakistan, beside the Silk Route from China).

POLO. Polo players are a breed apart. Top goal British players like Julian Hipwood are impassioned by the skill the game requires and the constant telepathy between player and horse. Hipwood started life as a soccer player but loves polo for the anticipation required for high-goal play and says 'You have to be three moves ahead, not just one.'

Now that polo has become such a social event, like racing, 'it matters not who won or lost' but how the spectators dress.

"My interpretation of style in dress and behaviour is entirely

based on the example of my father."

MAJOR RONALD FERGUSON

Visitors to the high-goal events of the season, usually sponsored by companies whose own image more than matches the glossy sophistication of that of the Polo Club, are faced with a dilemma. It's particularly difficult for men because for once, there *is* no uniform. (Well, there is, but it isn't so obvious as Derby Day or Ascot.) Although royalty is often present it's usually in an 'off-duty, just-popped-in-to-present-the-prizes' mood. (The Queen rarely wears a hat and the Princess of Wales has been observed without stockings.)

It's hard to take a cue from the experts: most of them seem to be playing and spectators can hardly waltz around in stretch white jodhpurs and boots. However, a watchful eye on the Royal Box of the Guards' Club at Smith's Lawn will provide some pointers. Smart, top quality blue blazer with crisp blue or white long-sleeved shirt and

THE CENTAURS POLO TEAM (ABOVE) WITH
HM THE QUEEN, AND RICHARD DUNHILL,
CHAIRMAN OF ALFRED DUNHILL LTD. AFTER
WINNING THE 1985 FINAL OF THE QUEEN'S CUP.

undemonstrative tie, grey flannel trousers and genuine panama hat if the weather is warm. Sensible lace-up Oxfords or half-brogues for treading in the divots (men in plimsolls and women in high heels look very silly) and a Barbour and plain black brolly if the weather is bad. Hang the Guards' Club Enclosure badge from the button hole on the blazer lapel and carry a decent pair of binoculars because, as everyone knows, the play always happens on the other side of the field. Dunhill Millenium or Cartier watch optional, depending on who is sponsoring the particular event.

Polo is probably one of the best sports at which to witness a transition from retrospective tradition to a new, international style in the Englishman's dress. Despite the high social rating, limitations in dress have not yet been set and practicality and comfort still rule the day. In addition, it's one of the few events where a man can wear 'sports' clothes to what is essentially a social event.

DERBY DAY AND ASCOT. Other events do mark the British racing calendar but Derby Day and Ascot are occasions when the Englisman once again reverts to full kit.

Morning dress (required in the Royal Enclosure at Ascot and in the enclosure of the Epsom Race Club) is a descendent of 1820s tail coats which were usually double-breasted and worn for riding as well as formal daywear. Scarlet was worn for hunting, dark green was the favourite colour for riding. By the 1860s, the morning coat was called a 'shooting coat' and was generally single-breasted with a longer waist and three to four buttons but by the turn of the century, this had again been modified and the single-button coat became popular. By the 1920s, tails were shorter (to the back of the knee) and cotton sleeve linings were added. Grey waistcoats, striped trousers and silk top hats became regular wear for smart weddings and ceremonial occasions. In a morning suit, trousers, waistcoat and coat generally match; the waistcoat is always single breasted and the trousers straight with no turn-up.

Morning dress must be one of the most difficult forms of ceremonial outfit the Englishman still chooses to wear. The single-button coat makes all but the most reed-like figure look plump and so does the waistcoat. Many seem too small for the body inside them and straining or gaping buttons

FULL MARKS HERE FOR BRAVADO,
WHICH IS WHAT STYLE IS ALL ABOUT.
OTHERS MIGHT FEEL THE BLAZER AND
TROUSERS ARE JUST A LITTLE TOO
NAUTICAL FOR THE EARTHIER BUSINESS
OF RACING BUT HOW YOU WEAR
CLOTHES IS AS IMPORTANT AS WHAT
YOU WEAR.

and waistcoats that ride high above the trousers are common sights among the squads of black and grey 'penguins'. The vast expanse of fly front is also a potential source of enormous embarrassment and few men can resist checking themselves with a reassuring pat after they've consumed several glasses of champagne. No matter how hot it becomes, the jacket must stay on, ties must stay tightened and braces hitched. Men must be about as comfortable as a Grenadier Guard in a heatwave – and as daft as women to allow tradition to dictate such eccentricity.

Most morning suits are hired these days. Make sure that the jacket and waistcoat are not too tight and the trousers not too long (just resting on the top of a well-polished Oxford). Avoid jackets which have a rather flash braided edge to the lapel and unless the occasion demands otherwise, choose a dark suit in preference to light grey because it will be

more flattering to the figure. Shirts are always white, tie usually plain grey with a grey suit, or discreetly patterned, with a top pocket handkerchief to match. Keep accessories plain as morning dress really requires no further embellishment.

CRICKET. Cricket is the last summer game left in England which began life in long trousers and has not yet degenerated into shorts. It is also, and has been since its Edwardian heyday, the sport in which everyone can participate enthusiastically without loss of dignity.

Dress has changed little over the years. Professional cricket is now 'accessorised' with warlike helmets which tend to give their wearers a 'mad dog' look, but amateur village cricket still adopts white trousers, white shirt and cricket boots like those that have been worn for more than a century.

Cricket pullovers are very often a work of art; beautiful garments interwoven with 'colours' from specialist retailer Kent and Curwen or, more personally, hand-knitted items toiled over by mother or girlfriend.

Blazers, sometimes adorned with club badge and cricket ties are still the emblems on the sidelines, though few ties are as distinctive as the traditional 'egg and tomato' of the MCC, the Marylebone Cricket Club.

Cricket history is starred with distinctive characters whose style has often included an element of eccentricity in personal appearance, from W.G. Grace's vast beard to Ian Botham's flowing golden locks.

Botham is a living cricket legend, the first player to have scored a century and taken eight wickets in a Test match and like Imran Khan (who in Oxbridge terms at least, is a 'Dark Blue'), his 'style' has spilled over from the cricket pitch into a life that mirrors *Boys Own Paper* heroism.

FEW CRICKET SPECTATORS TODAY
DRESS AS STYLISHLY AS THIS, MORE'S
THE PITY. MOST CONTEMPORARY STYLE
OFF THE PITCH SEEMS TO CONSIST IN
DOING THE MEXICAN WAVE BUT WHILE
THERE IS THE MCC, THERE IS HOPE.

To the experts, the game may have changed considerably but it still retains a dignity (expressed as much in dress) that is now lacking in tennis. It was only recently that jackets were allowed to be removed during heatwaves in the Pavilion at Lord's, but no matter how high the temperatures, collar and tie remains the rule. Standards are being preserved on the pitch. Away from it, Phil Edmonds is said to live in flares and it has been reported that he even wore cricket socks to his wedding.

TENNIS. Starched collars, long sleeves and turn-up trousers were once the order of the day in tennis. Even now, there is a club official who presides over the players' waiting-room at Wimbledon to make sure that competitors go on court on time and in 'correct dress', which must be predominantly white.

Jean René Lacoste was probably the inventor of a more relaxed tennis style for men. (It was also a Frenchman, Yvon Petra, who, in 1946, was the last champion to play in long trousers.) A champion player himself, Lacoste wanted a shirt which would be comfortable and practical for tennis players. He designed the classic shirt with long tail in 1926 and now the green crocodile has become synonymous with sport.

Lacoste's shirt originally had a stiff collar which enabled players also to wear it off court with a tie and jacket and thereby retain a degree of elegance. Nowadays, the 'touches of colour' permitted to players at Wimbledon have almost taken over the basic white as dignity is swapped for the riches of sponsorship in stripes and logos on shorts, shirts, socks, shoes, even headbands.

Björn Borg was one of the first to make a headband 'fashionable'. John McEnroe, by wrapping his forehead in a coloured kerchief, adapted the style with a gypsy wildness. Borg went on to design his own range of tennis wear and Pat Cash arrived to take up the headband and to pose with five pairs of Y-fronts, two clean shirts and a Scandinavian blonde in the pages of the *Tatler* magazine.

This is all a far cry from the days of 1877 when the All England Croquet and Lawn Tennis Club started the first lawn tennis championship and Wimbledon became the centre of the tennis world. Then, spectators paid a shilling to see the final and were as sedately dressed as the players.

GOOD TENNIS CLOTHES CARRY FEW
LOGOS. THEY ARE LIGHT AND
COMFORTABLE AND STYLE IS MORE A
MATTER OF BEHAVIOUR ON COURT
THAN THE CUT OF A PAIR OF SHORTS.

Spectators today reflect the 'informality' in the players' dress, except for the Royal Box where it is still formal. Jackets and ties are also required in the Members' Enclosure but elsewhere anything goes. Large notices request spectators not to remove their shirts within the club grounds but in hot weather they are rarely heeded. In one such summer heatwave in the Seventies, Joyce Grenfell objected mildly to the numbers of young men baring their torsos to the sun. 'It's so unfragrant,' she murmured with characteristic delicacy. How right she was. No man of style would ever 'expose' himself so blatantly so far from the water.

GOLF. Throughout its history, golf has been a popular sport. Prime Minister Balfour made it a 'fashionable' game in the Edwardian era when new courses were built with startling rapidity. Technical breakthrough came when the solid gutta-percha ball was replaced by an American invention, the rubber-cored Haskell ball in 1902, and golfing jokes were a constant source of inspiration to cartoonists of the period. But whereas cricket eroded the class differences, golf exacerbated them and the atmosphere of 'them and us' still reigns in some of the old-established clubs, such as the Royal and Ancient Golf Club of St Andrews, the 'home' of golf.

Situated by the sea and facing down four courses, including the famous Old Course, the R and A maintains tradition with a granite face. The Scots claim that golf was encouraged in St Andrews by medieval bishops because it lured the locals away from their archery practice. The Society of St Andrews golfers was founded in 1754 but it was not until 1834 that the club received royal patronage from William IV.

Women are still not allowed into the R and A. 'There aren't the facilities for them,' explains the present secretary, Michael Bonnalack. There are a few male preserves worth guarding and the R and A is one of them. Time seems to move very slowly here and crusty club members can still be seen stomping off down the fairway in the sort of dress that was popular before the World War – the first one.

Norfolk jackets, sports jackets and baggy knickerbockers were worn for golf in the early 1920s though some early cartoons show men wearing straight turn-up trousers and extraordinary checked jackets. The Prince of Wales was pictured playing golf in straight, turn-up trousers in 1922. He made the Fair-Isle pullover a popular piece of golf clothing and plus fours and jackets also came into vogue. Soft felt hats temporarily replaced the tight-fitting cap but by the 1930s the cap was back and so were trousers. Waist-length waterproof

JUST A WEE DOT AND A PAIR OF
PORRIDGE SOCKS. WARMTH COMES FIRST
ON THE WILDER SHORES OF GOLF.

jackets were introduced with zip fastenings at the side to prevent pouching when the golfer bent forward.

Golfers continued to play in shirt and tie until the Sixties when less conventional clothing became the norm for most sports and a general tendency towards informality made open-neck shirts and trousers acceptable 'casual' wear. Now golf, like tennis, has been hit by sponsorship fever and every visible item of clothing worn by the professionals usually carries someone's logo. For all that, golf still has an air of 'gentlemanly refinement'. Players are polite to each other and rarely embarrassingly demonstrative. They don't shout obscenities at the officials, and spectators are usually equally restrained, keeping their comment to polite applause. The presence of the Japanese has helped. A characteristically polite race, they have brought an honourable enthusiasm and good manners to the international events.

Some British players such as Nick Faldo maintain a certain style in clothing, wearing fine wool polo-neck pullovers or the classic polo shirt (though after their 1987 Ryder Cup victory, the English team were inclined to spoil the effect by throwing their clothing into the crowd), but Australian Rodger Davis has the greatest reputation for sartorial elegance on the course. His rainbow-coloured sweaters make eye-catching television. So do his natty plus-twos and long socks with his name clocked down each leg.

'Clothes are very important to a golfer. If you feel right, your chances of playing better are much greater,' he said at the Dunhill Cup in St Andrews in 1986, when Australia won for the second time in a row.

Comfort is obviously an essential element in the clothing of any sportsman but it plays an equally important part in a spectator's enjoyment of his day out. This is especially true on the windy courses of Scotland where golf assumes a national importance that lifts it into a 'social' league of its own.

Good shoes, preferably spiked, are essential. So is a warm, waterproof coat, hat, scarf and gloves. Once the course has been 'walked', there is the evening entertainment of the clubs and sponsorship marquees to be enjoyed. Here, shirt and tie are necessary and the blazer once again comes into its own. If you are being entertained by a sponsoring company, it

NICK FALDO, KNOWN FOR HIS STYLISH
GOLF AND HIS RELAXED, CASUAL
CLOTHING THAT PUTS COMFORT FIRST.

might be polite to wear a tie in their colours. This will go down well and probably ensure an invitation for the following year. As many club golfers are businessmen, a suit is almost out of place. Too many members spend their week in suits and the weekend should be marked out as different – relaxed, casual but still smart. Thermal underwear is a must for golfing events north of the border. In the day it will protect from the wind and rain of the great outdoors and in the evening it will prevent pneumonia caused by the howling gale that invariably whistles through the most glossy, centrally heated, glorified 'tent'.

SAILING. If racing and Ascot are the domain of the Queen, then sailing and Cowes belong to Prince Philip.

With the new mega-publicity given to the America's Cup (even the sails now have logos), sailing, like golf, has become a truly 'international' sport. The man who indulges must be courageous, transcontinental and rich. The bigger the

boat, the more appropriate the time-honoured description of sailing: 'like tearing up ten-pound notes under a cold shower'.

Sailing in British waters attracts two kinds of people. The socially aware who turn up for odd summer weekends and are always available for Cowes Week, and the demented who race every series, are impervious to cold and wet and have livers lined with cast iron.

The Cowes regatta is a chance to see the British naval spirit that won the Battle of Trafalgar. Members of the Royal Yacht Squadron turn out in full naval kit – double-breasted, shining buttons, pips on display.

Members have three official uniforms: mess jacket with dark blue waistcoat and trousers for very formal occasions, reefer jacket (blazer) with silver buttons for less formal wear, and reefer with black buttons (with Squadron cypher) for 'undress'.

MORE JOLLY SAILOR CLOTHING FOR
THE LANDLUBBER WHO ONLY TAKES TO
THE WATER OCCASIONALLY. REAL
RACING MEN HAVE A LESS IMMACULATE
STYLE WHICH IS VERY UNPHOTOGENIC.

Cowes has a variety of yacht clubs but the Royal Yacht Squadron holds the cream. The Duke of Edinburgh is Admiral and among the members are a number of Conservative sailors including Edward Heath. 'Blackballing' (the practice of placing a black ball in a ballot box to reject a candidate) is still used though dress regulations seem to have relaxed a little as members are now sometimes allowed to drink on the deck of the club in sailing gear. Like many London clubs, the Royal Yacht Squadron 'tolerates' women, but only on certain days and in certain parts of the club. The big social night at Cowes is the Squadron Dance, a ritzy black-tie affair which sets the 'tone' for the regatta.

Sailing is a complicated sport and new spectators often find it hard to work out what is happening. The best way to enjoy a race is on a boat, but if forced to stay on land, it's wise to confess complete ignorance and stay by the bar. For this kind of activity, wear a blazer (*not* with nautical buttons), collar and tie. For those on board a little reconnaissance is essential. Oilskins may be vital for a wet race in a

small boat but they can look pretty silly on the rear deck of a motorised gin palace. Plimsolls or rubber-soled 'deck shoes' are essential as boats are wet, slippery places and it's worth remembering that it's *always* colder at sea. Choose a warm pullover, a waterproof jacket and light cotton trousers instead of jeans for informal sailing – denim holds water longer. Polo shirts and classic white shorts are regulation for pottering about in harbour in warm-water sailing.

THE FREE STYLERS

Between 1979 and 1985, sales of sports clothing and footwear increased by 164 per cent at a time when the total clothing market was in decline. A large part of this increase must have been in ski-wear because this has now become a section of the 'fashion industry'.

'Style' on the slopes no longer refers to the elegance with which a double pike is performed. It means wearing the right designer label and the very latest in 'Tecno' – technical man-made materials.

Skiing has always been for the daring and slightly unconventional. The English country gentleman addicted to hunting, shooting and fishing at home found it as remote as the lower classes did. It was left to the 'adventurers' in life and later, the daring young things of the Twenties, to be the first to colonise the Continental slopes and establish the British at the forefront of what has become a fashionable sport.

Strangely enough, the clothes these daredevils of the slopes wore were very similar to country uniform for the more traditional pursuits of hunting, shooting etc. Pre-1920s ski kit included boots and breeches with oiled stockings, topped by a Norfolk tweed jacket or a Burberry's gaberdine coat. Soon however, London department stores were opening 'Alpine Departments' where emphasis was placed on 'correct kit' which meant that doubt had already set in. The Continentals were fighting back and the British found themselves out on a snowclad limb in their nylon stretch trousers and dark blue windcheaters which Moss Bros promised were 'absolutely right'.

Package holidays arrived to revolutionise British skiing and the pre-paid fortnight, or even the skiing weekend, was open to all. The cry went up to 'Spot the C and A' and the

STYLE ON THE SLOPES MEANS WEARING
THE RIGHT DESIGNER LABEL AND
LOOKING AS IF YOUR PERFORMANCE
CAN MATCH YOUR OUTFIT. COMFORT
SHOULD ALWAYS COME FIRST.

Englishman gave in to the foreign designs on his body. (C and A is a Dutch company.)

Salopettes faded from view and Microfibre came in. Tecno man raced down the slopes in a Swedish, Japanese or West German one-piece wearing brightly coloured boots like Superman. Après-ski took on an 'international' look in cashmere polo-necks and slacks. But it was the accessories that really changed things for the Englishman. Out in the frozen wastes of foreign parts, he could happily slap on the moisturiser without feeling effeminate. He could pack his bum bag or brightly coloured rucksack with tanning products, moisture cream, lip-salve and feel that these were as essential a part of his equipment as the flask of Dunhill Old Master whisky. Off the slopes, he happily shaved and showered in distinctive, subtle fragrances that would have taken years of acclimatisation at home and shampooed and conditioned his hair flattened by woolly hat or headband, with uncharacteristic enthusiasm.

Suddenly, men discovered toiletries and sturdy types from Manchester with proper jobs in British Telecom were swopping opinions on skin creams and moisturisers and how to prevent the cold freezing the razor rash.

Accessories became polished. The right gloves (no mittens), corresponding with the ski outfit. Glacier glasses for the super-sophisticated, funky-coloured goggles for the less serious. Helmet hats and handwraps for 'Eurostyle', earmuffs, Walkmans and bobbly, woolly 'favourite' hats for the Hooray Henrys. Colour-toning bum bags (called fanny-packs in America) with particular emphasis on banana yellow and mango.

Now that they are fashion items, ski clothes are constantly changing but for the man determined to stay ahead of the rest, certain elements of style have already emerged:

Ski-style. Hand in glove with the latest accessories which offer more hi-tech protection for the downhill races.

OUT	IN
Bobble hats	Sleek, simple one-piece
Walkman	Fluorescents and acids
Cherry brandy	Factor 20
Pastels	Black and brown
Separates	Thermals
Luhta Mango	Gloves
Fluorescent zinc cream	Lycra stretch
Mittens	Dunhill Old Master whisky
Shouting at your female companion (unless she's wearing a Fergie headband or a cowl)	Radar reflectors

CROSS COUNTRY. Once considered the skiing alternative for geriatrics and the unsupple, cross country is now appreciated for its fast, energy-sapping athleticism. Less exciting perhaps than pounding down the black runs or mogul bashing but just as physically exhausting, as any runner in the Eingedin marathon will confirm.

Cross-country clothing is less *chi-chi* than the Alpine variety. It's extremely warm work and performed at lower altitudes so super-insulation can be too much. The traditionalists still ski in Tyrolean-type salopettes with bodywarmer vest or jacket that they can unpeel as the temperature rises. The serious racers go for the shiny-tight lycra suit with the sprayed-on look, zip channels that provide insulation in all the right places, double-sealed seams, outer layers with Thinsulate linings and a style cut to allow maximum freedom of movement. Never dress up in all this unless you are about to live up to it. There's nothing so uncool as a chap in a tight one-piece who hasn't yet found his rhythm, and in cross country, you can't just stand around by the chair lifts and admire the view.

BOOT WORK. Experts say skiers at the middle performance level have the hardest time buying boots. The top class know what they want and go for it. The beginner

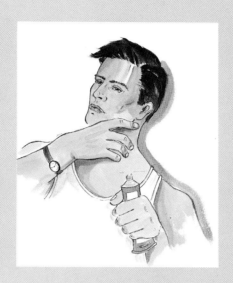

SKINCARE NOTES
SUN ON THE SLOPES

*N*ever underestimate the winter sun in snow conditions at high altitudes. The ultra-violet intensity rises in clear weather by up to 100 per cent for every 1,000 metres elevation. Even in cloudy weather UV radiation increases at altitudes above 2,000 metres. Cold affects skin as adversely as heat and skiers moving at speed attract skin temperatures at well below freezing point. It may be −10°C in the atmosphere but −35°C on the face in a fast downhill run.

Stealing the girlfriend's Nivea will not help. Most moisturisers contain a high degree of water (hence their name) which can 'freeze' on the face. Look for water-free products containing oils which leave a thin, insulating film on the skin. Lips dry out easily and cracked, sore mouths are uncomfortable and unsexy. Protect with a 'total block' (check packaging to see it guarantees against UV rays) – also useful for nose and eyelids. Fluorescent zinc creams or dead-white are going out of style. Après-ski, avoid stinging after-shaves on tender skin. Choose the alcohol-free type or a soothing moisture cream.

settles for ski-hire or a sales bargain. First thing is to make the most of good sales advice. Ask, try and compare. 'Bend zer knees' is also important as flexing affects performance and fit. 'Flex' appeal is paramount, certainly more essential to the serious skier than colour choice. Rear-entry boots are in, overlaps are fading.

Beach Style

The young, British male has never been the same since he discovered windsurfing. Now he spends his weekends zooming across gravel pits in England, swathed in rubber latex from windsurfing hood to Typhoon Calothermic boot.

Windsurfing in England appeals to the masochistic element in the British male in the same way as kicking the shins out of an opponent on a frozen-hard rugby pitch. (It also appeals to females who probably enjoyed hockey at school.)

Windsurfers are tough. When they aren't risking hypothermia out on the water, they're usually doing something relaxing, like mountain biking. They watch their diets and tend to be vegetarian. Style is essential. The professional windsurfing man may not always 'do it standing up' but he *always* does it in style.

Fashion, Image and Colour are important. No one would be seen dead in a plain black wetsuit. Offbeat, psychedelic colours are the thing, the brighter the better, in Ripstop/Gitane Blue, Lime Green, or a combination of both, planing through the waves like exotic butterflies.

Body awareness is high. Windsurfers are lean and keen and popular with the women. They have a wardrobe of clothing from the five-millimetre-thick 'winter steamer' to the double-pocketed, totally trendy surf shorts worn with a thin cotton T-shirt to stop the 'wind chill'.

Like skiers, surfmen appreciate the finishing touch of the totally right accessory. Theft deterrents for sailboards, go-faster micro-grooved tape and, most important, the totally original, water-resistant wristwatch, featuring calendar, lap memory, second time zone, three-mode countdown timer, luminescent hands and a five-year battery.

BEACH COMBERS. We are an island race and the Englishman who doesn't participate in watersports has a hard time on the beach. Unable to throw himself into frenzied

SUN ON THE SHORE

*W*ater reflects light and adds to burning. So does wind, even on dull days. Protect the face with a high-protection cream when sailing, or wear a hat. The area around the eyes and the nose is particularly vulnerable. On the body, the shoulders tend to burn easily – less fat over the bone structure. Spray washes off sun-tanning products so reapply creams frequently. Oils give less protection against UV light and on their own, they do not promote tanning. It's the 'photo-active' ingredients that do the work. The well-oiled bronzed look is only for Posers. It goes with the Bleached Blonde Beach Bum style and piña coladas. Look for a high-factor waterproof cream and reapply frequently. Sun beds do not filter out harmful rays. They can give a pale body a start but protect face, wear goggles and never wear aftershave or fragrance – they may cause allergic reaction.

activity on or near the water, he has to rely on looking ultra-smooth but in a laid-back, unhairy way in case he gets mistaken for an Italian waiter.

Good news are the 'jams' that first appeared on the horizon from Los Angeles in 1987. Not trousers or shorts, but somewhere between the two, they were an updated version of Baden Powell Gone Eye-Blindingly Colourful. They instantly appealed to the Englishman who hankered after the shorts of his schoolboy days and also helped hide the knobbly British knee but, in general, designer swimwear for men has been slow to develop in the UK.

Today's Englishman is surprisingly sedate on the sands. In Edwardian times, the men bathed 'au naturel', while women crouched in voluminous shifts and parked themselves in bathing cars at the other end of the beach. Gwen Raverat, a young middle-class lady from Cambridgeshire (and grand-daughter of Charles Darwin) described in her book *Period Piece* how she wickedly glimpsed the young men leaping into the waters of the Fens and thought them rather lovely – slender and pink. She probably also envied their freedom from the women's dress of the day which she found caused 'restraint and pain'.

Men continued to bathe nude in Hyde Park until the beginning of the century. Oxford University, true to form, continued the practice even longer at a private site called 'Parson's Pleasure'.

Early twentieth-century swimwear was very unappealing. Men wore two-part bathing costumes, made of cotton with a Y-shaped back, which did little to enhance the British figure. Trunks first appeared in the 1930s and from then on things got increasingly brief.

Tight G-strings have never had any style. They were too emphatic on the well-made and ridiculous on the under-endowed. Somehow, the great British bottom wasn't designed to be highlighted in a shining square of bright blue nylon and the return of the 'long' shorts was a relief to most – comfortable and stylish in good colours.

There are still some of us who feel that twentieth-century men are right not to reveal all like the bare-breasted female. Male nudity may be 'classical' but it only suits the really sculptured.

BODY BUILDING

No man can hit the beach in style if he is an eight-stone weakling or an eighteen-stone whale. Men like to think they have fewer weight problems than women but their fat just collects in different places. The key to good form is regular exercise and good diet. According to The Economist Intelligence Unit, the sports boom of the Eighties has had less to do with people actually playing sport than with individuals improving their fitness with personal exercise programmes. That's the good news. The bad news is that the fit are still in a minority. Jogging, rowing machines, home gyms, all help improve physical fitness but rippling glutes and lats also require good nutrition.

Main types of foods are carbohydrates, fats and proteins. Carbohydrates provide the body with a ready source of energy for all its activities (e.g. muscular). Simple carbohydrates include glucose and fructose. Complex carbohydrates are found in the starchy part of potatoes, peas, grains and beans and, on their own, are low in calories per unit volume. Fats are also a source of energy and dietary fats belong to two broad categories – saturated and unsaturated. The first kind are opaque and solid, like butter or lard. Unsaturated fats are clear and liquid – like sunflower oil. Fats have a higher calorie content than sugars and can contribute to circulatory disease. Proteins perform the body's repair work. They are part of the connective tissue and present in every cell of the body. Proteins are made from hydrogen, carbon, oxygen and nitrogen. The latter isn't stored in the body and is needed on a daily basis. A good diet therefore is rich in carbohydrates and proteins and low in fats.

Good sources of carbohydrates: wholemeal bread, pasta, brown rice, potatoes, whole grains, root vegetables, peas, beans, lentils.

Good protein sources: eggs, fish, poultry – red meat is harder for the system to digest.

Fats are found in most foods – fish, meat, dairy foods, nuts and grains – so cutting out fried foods, cakes and biscuits will not leave the body short. Many men believe that giving up bread and potatoes will make them lose weight yet wholemeal bread and potatoes are relatively low in calories. Far better to give up alcohol – it contains one and three-quarter times the calorific value of either carbohydrates or proteins.

CHAPTER FIVE

THE FORMAL ENGLISHMAN

"Real dress style is actually quite conventional but it just has that twist of something different. It's never studied or worked on and it often has a touch of eccentricity. Prince Philip has it, but so does comedian Dave Allen. Mark Birley, Dougie Fairbanks and the Duke of Beaufort all have it. It's a blend of fastidiousness, a good eye for detail – and charm."

LORD LICHFIELD

Real style goes beyond dress. It reflects the whole man and his position in society. Dress is itself an expression of social change which always goes in cycles. Each new season brings another variation on an established theme but the constituent parts remain remarkably similar.

Recent fashion in films has seen the influence of an elegance which had its heyday in the Edwardian period but the 1890s invite comparisons with our own period which go beyond the subject of how to dress well.

Then, as now, money was the yardstick of success. Get-rich-quick schemes enthralled the Edwardians as much as public share offers have gripped the current imagination. The cash-down climate also gave rise to a series of flamboyant financial swindles and speculators of the period as, for example, the notorious Whittaker Wright.

The nation was obsessed with its health. Spas took the place of the modern health club and 'Swedish Drill' was the Edwardian answer to aerobics. The use of contraceptives was on the rise amongst the middle class and syphilis was the sexual scourge of the day.

Edwardian women discovered new economic freedom as they entered careers as shop girls, typists and telephone operators. They were more sporty and played golf, croquet and hockey and were keen bicyclists. They were also independently minded and intensely political, and as bricks crashed through cabinet ministers' windows in demand of women's rights, they shattered the old family order.

In contrast to this starkness, was a more romantic nature. Women devoured the novels of Elinor Glyn and the personal columns of the newspapers were filled with messages of love. Clothes reflected this romanticism, not least male evening dress which mirrored the court finery of earlier times.

On the rare sunny day in England, the Englishman bursts forth from his chrysalid to dazzle the more subdued with an outfit which is positively joyful. This is real style – the nerve to stand out in a crowd and the ability to enjoy it.

The style arbiter of the age was Mrs Humphrey, who laid down the law in her book *Manners for Men*, first published in 1897. A gentleman was distinguished by his 'ease and aplomb' in good society but above all, he had to have a good character. 'Gentleness and moral strength combined must be the salient characteristics of the gentleman,' she wrote. Kindness, affection and thoughtfulness were also recommended.

Much the same applies today as the best contemporary heroes have a social style expressed in consideration for others. Few people now care if you know how to seat fourteen at dinner, address the Archbishop of Malta or answer a formal invitation to tea. In today's world, rigid rules of behaviour are as superfluous as rigid rules of dress but no one can claim to have style if they neglect basic good manners.

Formal dress still gives a man an instant sense of occasion. The Englishman remains an expert at dressing up, whether for formal sporting events (*see previous chapter*), for weddings, for balls or, occasionally, for opera. Few things complete the transformation so well as an element of social style.

Evening Dress

Nothing looks so out of place as the wrong colour or cut in evening clothes. As most wardrobes will only include one dinner suit, it pays eventually to have the best.

JACKET. Choose black or midnight blue wool with barathea or grosgrain lapels. Satin and velvet lapels can quickly look old-fashioned. The old rule was shawl collar with double-breasted, peaked lapels with single-breasted but shawl collars are increasingly popular for both styles of jacket. They add a softer outline but unless cut deep and low, can make a portly figure look even stouter. As with any suit, check the fit carefully to see that seams fitting sleeve to jacket rest at the natural edge of the shoulder and that the jacket collar hugs the back of the neck properly. Length is important to help 'proportion' the trousers. The jacket should usually come to

THIS MAN IS A STAR. HE HAS MANAGED
TO FASTEN HIS BOW TIE SINGLE-HANDED
AND IN THE DARK.

just below the buttocks. Eventually, the material will age and sometimes takes on a 'greenish' colour. Watch out for this if buying secondhand as there is no way to get rid of the problem.

White 'party' jackets are popular alternatives to a black dinner jacket and can be worn with the same dark trousers. Once again, choose a plain style in preference to anything with noticeable detail that might date more quickly.

TROUSERS. Side braid is a relic of regimental uniform and generally looks better in a matt material which does not attract the eye too much. Button flies make a more elegant alternative to zips but braces should be button-down, preferably on to a peaked back. Resist the temptation to hoist braces too high so that trousers ride up at the back. They should sit at waist level and hang straight to rest on the front of the shoe.

WAISTCOATS. Rich colours such as claret and midnight blue or paisley patterns add an attractive element of style to a dinner suit but waistcoats should first and foremost fit flat across the stomach. Never leave the top button undone or let the bottom button gape to show a gap between shirt and trousers. The style of the waistcoat depends a good deal on the style of dinner jacket. Shawl collars look well in matching waistcoat and jacket but in general, those with fuller figures should stick to peaked lapels which have a more slimming effect. They should also avoid backless waistcoats attached at waist level with a belt and buckle as these tend to 'ride up' over a capacious stomach. Avoid bright colours if overweight – they draw attention to the problem. White cotton piqué waistcoats are simple, elegant and suit most figures. Look for important details like tiny mother-of-pearl buttons. Pockets should be small and lie completely flat.

CUMMERBUNDS. The cummerbund makes an elegant alternative to the waistcoat and particularly suits the tall and slender figure. Always wear with the folds pointing upwards

TWO STYLES OF EVENING WEAR.

and don't fasten too tightly. Bright colours and patterns will draw attention to an expanding waistline but a black cummerbund helps 'extend' the waist up from the trousers.

SHIRTS. Keep to a simple style and avoid frills and too much decoration. Finely pressed pleats look elegant as does a contrasting front in cotton piqué. White or cream is still more stylish than a coloured evening shirt and the best material is fine cotton or silk. Avoid synthetics.

Studs are preferable to buttons but keep them small and simple. Wing collars are usually worn with tails but current 'rules' for evening dress are frequently adapted and wing collars also make a stylish alternative to the turn-down collar with the ordinary dinner jacket. Some men claim wing collars are more comfortable as they don't catch the neck when leaning forward. Turn-back cuffs are best for shirt sleeves with studs to match the shirt front.

"I define style as having the confidence to express oneself

in everything one does."
LORD GRADE

TIES. Bow ties have their own special style. They have always been fashionable and always regarded with suspicion by those who consider them difficult to tie. In fact the bow is similar to a reef knot (also used to tie shoe laces) and quite simple (*see illustration*).

Pre-knotted bows lack style because they do not 'sit' properly and they look so obviously artificial. The usual material for bow ties is either silk or barathea. Silk can be rather slippery and a little more difficult to tie.

SHOES. Patent pumps with grosgrain bows are still popular but a pair of plain black patent Oxfords look just as well. Black socks are a must but choose a pair that come to the knee as nothing looks worse than a gap between ankles and the trouser bottom.

HOW TO TIE A BOW TIE

1 TAKE BOTH ENDS AND MAKE A FOLD IN THE RIGHT, LOOPING THE OTHER END UNDER AND UP.

2 MAKE ANOTHER 'HALF BOW' WITH THE LEFT END AND FOLD IT ACROSS THE FRONT OF THE TIE.

3 FEED THE SECOND LOOP BEHIND THE FIRST.

4 PULL BOTH ENDS THROUGH AND CHECK THAT THE ENDS MEET (IF THEY DON'T YOU HAVE TO START AGAIN).

5 NEATEN THE BOW BY PRESSING FORWARD WITH THE THUMBS.

EVENING MANNERS

*V*olumes have been written on precedence and protocol but few contemporary occasions require much consideration of such finer points of social behaviour.

However, knowledge of a few guidelines can make a man feel more relaxed. If uncertain, always ask about 'appropriate' dress. Beware of invitations to 'come as you are' from senior colleagues at work or those you don't know very well as it can be far less casual than it sounds. Most evening invitations require a tie.

Do try to arrive on time. Unpunctuality can ruin a dinner and is unforgivable for formal occasions. If it is a large formal party, always greet the host and hostess first. Less important today are correct introductions, though you should wait to be introduced to really distinguished guests and not introduce yourself.

Check the table plan carefully in advance at a formal dinner if only to avoid the embarrassment of having to hunt for your place when everyone else has already found theirs.

Talk to both your neighbours and try not to neglect an older woman for the stunning blonde on your other side.

The old rule of working from the outside in still applies in coping with a lot of cutlery, but don't worry if you make mistakes. It is a worse crime to pile the plate with too much food. At a small dinner party, it may leave less for others and could mean you are still eating when everyone else is finished and waiting for the next course.

Formal dinners can be long and as it isn't polite to leave the table before the end, it pays to pace your drinking carefully. Smoking between courses spoils any meal and if you wish to smoke afterwards, it's considerate to ask your host and your companion guests' permission first.

Always write or phone to say thank you the next day. This is also the best moment to give flowers as if you arrive at a dinner party carrying them, it means the hostess has to rush off and find a vase instead of greeting her other guests. In some countries, it is considered more polite to send flowers before a dinner party. Don't take a bottle to a formal party unless specifically asked to do so.

WEDDING STYLE

The most formal outfit for bridegrooms (and ushers) is Morning Dress. It is only necessary to own one if you are also going to use it for other events such as Ascot and formal Balls, otherwise, it is more economical to hire. Morning dress comprises:

- Tailed coat, often grey, especially in summer. Black always looks more elegant and flatters the figure more than grey but is often considered too sombre.
- Grey striped trousers (no turn-ups).
- Grey waistcoat, usually double-breasted.
- Grey tie or sometimes a grey cravat.
- White shirt with turn-down collar.
- Black socks and shoes and white handkerchief, plainly folded and tucked in the top pocket.
- Toppers are best discarded as they are impossible to wear in wedding cars and have to be carried everywhere. Gloves are also optional.

The best man, bride's father, groom's father and ushers all wear the same as the groom.

Formal suits are now frequently worn at weddings. Choose a light grey or dark blue, preferably with matching waistcoat, plain or striped material but no checks or tweeds. Trousers look better straight with no turn-ups. Choose a plain white shirt in finest sea-island cotton with turn-down collar and wear with a silk tie 'matched' with a silk handkerchief to blend with the colours in the suit. Keep socks plain, in navy, black or grey to match the trousers and choose plain-styled black shoes.

Buttonholes are a matter of personal taste. Carnations are traditional but old-fashioned pinks look more original than the hot-house, artificially coloured carnations of today.

Being Best Man can involve much more than simply making a funny speech, so choose yours carefully. The choice is always the sole prerogative of the bridegroom and though it is normal to select a single man, the final selection

MORNING DRESS.

BODY NOTES

*H*owever formal or informal the wedding, it is a good idea to look tidy. If you need a haircut, have it several days in advance so that the neck doesn't look newly shaved. If it is your wedding try to have the stag party a few nights beforehand to give yourself time to recover.

The night before, lay out all your clothes and check that everything is in order – no buttons missing, broken shoe laces and nothing that looks very 'new' (wear a shirt that has been washed once to remove any stiffness). Don't forget clean socks or underwear.

On the day, shave early and try not to swamp yourself in potent aftershave. Wash your hair well ahead of time and let it dry naturally so that it doesn't look frizzy. Don't slick it down with anything shiny. Don't forget to use an under-arm deodorant and to give teeth an extra good clean. If this all sounds too obvious for words, remember even the most stylish can lose their nerve under matrimonial pressure.

HONEYMOONS SHOULD BE HOLIDAYS,
CLOTHES RELAXED AND COMFORTABLE.

should fall on someone you can trust to deal efficiently with all the arrangements and any emergencies which might arise.

The above outlines only the more traditional approach to weddings but whatever you wear, discuss it first with your female partner to make sure you both hit the right note. The best weddings are those which everyone enjoys, especially the two main participants, so make sure you feel comfortable in your clothes and try everything on well in advance.

STYLISH PROPS FOR THE HONEYMOON. Forget the coloured condoms and the side-split boxer shorts with roses on them. Whether you are using the honeymoon suite in the

Ritz or camping under canvas on a hillside, you will need one essential item – a memorable dressing gown.

It should not be part of your usual wardrobe and nothing like the old woollen dressing gown you had at boarding school. It must be opulent and tactile in rich-coloured silk or thick white cashmere, distinguished for its sheer extravagance and luxury.

No matter how well you already know your partner it will make a lasting impression and establish you as a man of definitive taste.

New Style Occasions

Dressing for today's occasions goes beyond the traditional. Television is now part of everyday life and magnifies the 'style' of those who feature on it. There are also other 'occasions' of which a man needs to be aware. Of these, the role of Wife Supporter and potential lover are the most important.

DRESSING FOR THE TELEVISION INTERVIEW The television interview can provide the big break. This is an age of instant experts and everyone is required, at some time or other, to comment. Those who manage to do so with panache get remembered, though often what is said is secondary to how it is 'projected'.

Rule one is be prepared. There may not be time to rush home and change the tie or shirt. Rule two is to *look* unprepared, or at least busy – as if you've just been dragged from the front line, or Number 10 Downing Street, but never from the mirror in the men's room. The style of the Englishman on television, as in everything else, is unstudied. The desired effect is to project knowledge of any subject with confident nonchalance. Clothes which look too carefully chosen are as damning as an over-rehearsed speech.

If the programme is a political one, the dark serious suit is a must. Avoid large stripes, bold checks or houndstooth patterns and bold colours on shirt fronts, as they 'strobe'. This means the lines on clothes merge with the lines which make up television pictures resulting in collective migraine among the viewing population.

In dressing for the chat show, men have a great advantage over women. The margin for error is less wide.

Women will dress like Cinderella appearing for her first ball. Call it 'Dallas', 'Dynasty', 'Power' dressing, the result is too theatrical. The Englishman's wardrobe usually contains few alarming 'fashion' items but he can quickly achieve the same display of style-deprivation by wearing brightly coloured socks, a fluorescent tie, or snakeskin shoes.

How you dress depends on the image you want to create, which, in turn, should be a reflection of your *own* style. Chat show hosts on British TV tend to err on the side of the formal – jackets and ties (high heels and huge earrings for the ladies) designed to give an air of 'relaxed formality' but looking instead stiff and uneasy. The other extreme is the Frank Bough cardigan.

Settle for a comfortable compromise. The navy blue blazer will not let you down. Wear with light trousers and open-neck shirt in summer (add a silk scarf if age is over thirty and the neck is either thick or wrinkly), socks that tone with trousers, and tennis or deck shoes for a touch of casual athleticism.

In winter, add darker flannels or cord trousers to the blazer and a polo-neck sweater in a fine ply (television studios can be warm) and toning socks with a smart, well-polished pair of Oxfords.

"The most important thing is to be yourself and wear what

pleases you, not your audience. Don't try to construct a false

image – it lacks credibility."
MICHAEL BUERK, *BBC Newsman*

This is the background. Classic, stylish and as plain as possible so that viewers remember your face. Bright colours and fancy patterns detract from the face (though this is worth remembering if you have a dreadful hangover). They can also clash with the set. Pay particular attention to any use of 'colour separation overlay' in the programme – where pictures are projected on to a screen behind you, as in news programmes. If your shirt is too close to the colour of the screen you may find the picture displayed on your chest.

MAKE AN IMPRESSION BY LOOKING AS
IF YOU'VE JUST DROPPED IN FROM
ANOTHER APPOINTMENT SOMEWHERE
ALTOGETHER SMARTER.

Be aware of details which the camera will merci-lessly expose. No glimpses of hairy ankle between socks and trouser leg for example (most important on the chat show where the camera often draws back for a full-length picture). Make sure hair and – most important – hands, are clean. Television magnifies gestures and if you use your hands when you talk (and most people do), nails will get noticed. They must be clean and well-trimmed unless your hands deliber-ately reflect a rugged profession.

The best way to make a good impression is to be yourself. For those in politics this is nearly impossible. For the rest, take advice from newsman Michael Buerk (who has never worn a padded shoulder in his life) and keep your credibility when all around are losing theirs.

Finally, if blazers and flannels sound boring remem-ber the more colourful the background, the less likely that the public will remember you and what you have to say. But if brightly coloured clothes are the way you usually express yourself, that's fine. Wear your purple cloak and diving mask for your TV debut. Just don't expect anyone to listen carefully to your views on the Eurotunnel at the same time.

DRESSING TO SUPPORT THE SUCCESSFUL WIFE

Women are now everywhere in a man's world. In such circumstances it takes a man of real character and considerable style to play a supporting role without letting the Little Woman metaphorically castrate him.

The Englishman is a natural expert in the art of walking two steps behind. He mirrors this style better than anyone in the world. He has the Duke of Edinburgh as role model, a tradition of classic tailoring and needs little else to play the part perfectly.

Being a good Wife Supporter requires age, experi-ence and a reasonably good figure. A well-cut Savile Row suit can transform most shapes but there is no doubt that it still looks best on the man with military bearing. Keep shirts plain

THIS LUCKY LADY HAS TWO
SUPPORTERS – ONE TO HOLD HER DRINK,
THE OTHER TO UNWRAP PRESENTS

and classic and stick to the institutional tie. Wear traditional lace-up Oxfords, dark socks and classic coats and hats and keep accessories minimalist but important.

Carry a good fountain pen, for example. 'She' may need it when signing formal documents. This gives the Wife Supporter an opportunity to show that he is better organised than the assorted young men who crowd round a woman of substance and that he is useful in his own right. Also carry a clean white cotton handkerchief (in addition to the one in the top pocket). Never carry an umbrella. Leave that to the flunkies or the security men. Dashing alongside with a raised brolly looks too servile and the real Wife Supporter *never* looks servile. He may be second in line and he knows his place but he also knows that it is never that of a 'servant'. This distinguishes him from all those other supporting roles such as 'lover' and 'walker' which are far beneath his peculiar status.

The 'Official' Wife Supporter, he who is subjected to the scrutiny of the public glare glancing off his wife, never smokes in public, has affairs or talks to the Press. He is a scandal-proof family man and when his grown-up children misbehave, he regards it with the same nonchalance as when his wife does something stupid. In other words, he always remains loyal.

Loyalty is his stock in trade. He never sniggers when the Wife makes a fool of herself in public. (If she stumbles over a speech, mixes up names and countries, forgets who has a knighthood and who hasn't he simply looks vague and deaf.) He never complains about his role, his family or the number of ridiculous cocktail parties he is expected to attend. The words 'kiss and tell' are Greek to him and he stonewalls the reptiles of the world's Press with an unruffled ease that leaves them speechless.

However, he sometimes exerts himself into temporary prominence. This in no way endangers his position as Official Wife Supporter. If anything, it is enhanced because it shows that he has a mind of his own, albeit one bent on things other than his wife's work. For this reason, he never troubles himself to comment on what she does or how she does it. When he feels the need to express an opinion, it is on something remote such as the preservation of Pandas in Outer Mongolia or renovating golf courses in the Falkland Islands.

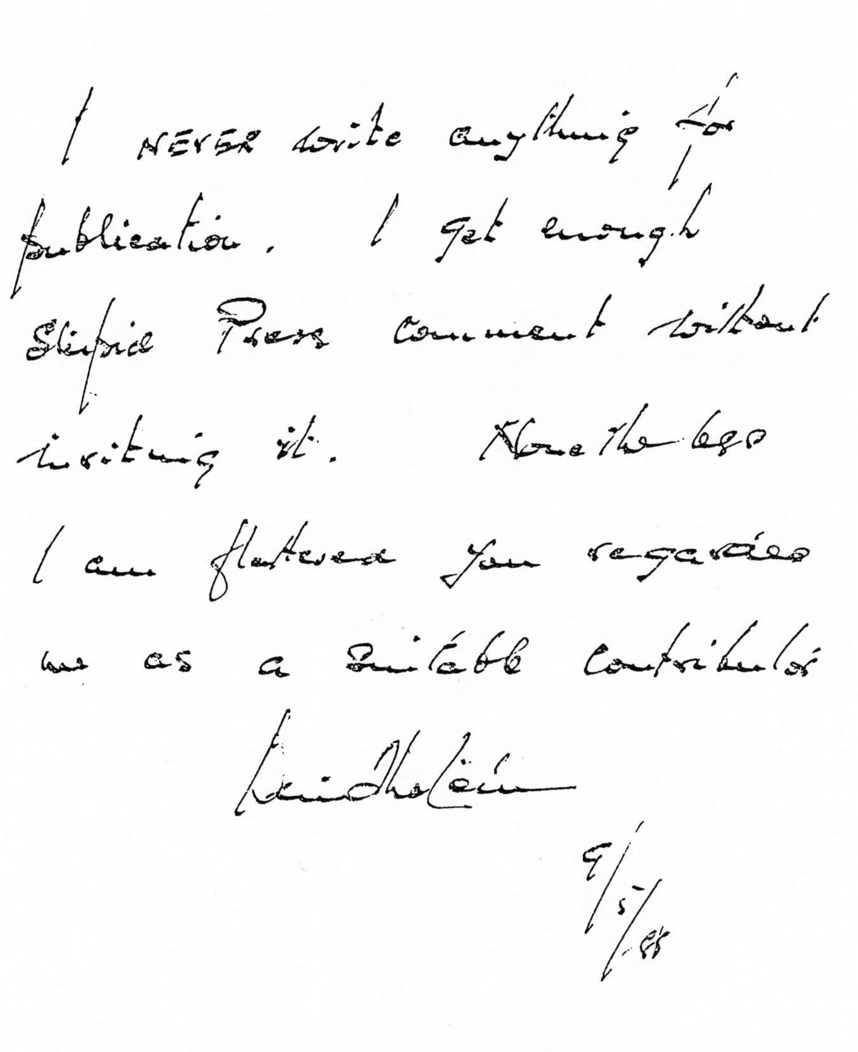

I NEVER write anything for publication. I get enough stupid Press comment without writing it. None the less I am flattered you regarded me as a suitable contributor

[signature]

9/5/85

He speaks on this with passion and authority, gets quoted in the *Daily Telegraph* and forgotten about a few days later.

This exemplifies his role. To be so far above the ordinary turmoil of life, that he becomes almost faceless. This enables him to avoid being a 'personality' and preserve a degree of normality in his life. His clothes reflect this. They are plain, solid, conservative, an outward expression of his confident belief that however odd the goings-on around him (the wife can appear in 'power shoulders' but it will not alter his own style), he remains, at heart, his own master.

DRESSING FOR LUNCH WITH THE MISTRESS

Young men have always valued the companionship of older women. The 'toy boy' syndrome is just a new expression of a tradition that the Englishman, at least, has always enjoyed.

Female British royalty has favoured the younger lover. Elizabeth I was considerably older than Robert, Earl of Essex who 'enjoyed many favours' at her court and Princess Margaret has also shown a preference for the younger man as companion.

At the top end of the market, the older Mistress is a valuable asset. She is discreet, elegant, usually independently wealthy and unlikely to throw tantrums when the affair ends. She is also rare. Cheap imitations abound, from flashy filmstar glamour to second-rate socialite. They suit the man who wants to show off but as the Englishman with style rarely wishes to do this, he will take trouble to look for the genuine article.

He finds her at country house parties, in private boxes at operas and occasionally at a summer sporting event, such as Henley or Ascot. Introductions are essential. Real women of affluence know their worth and do not take kindly to being approached with an obvious pick-up line. This helps differentiate them from their imitators who will happily go out with the 'rough trade'. The upper-crust mistress is rarely seen without a title and can recognise a gentleman from an easy fifty paces.

For this reason, she prefers Englishmen with background, breeding and style. However, she can also be persuaded by someone more transatlantic and is impressed by body language. She may be French herself, or part Italian or something exotic from South America, so is aware of 'shape' as well as 'form'.

If you have a good body emphasise it. Chose a subdued (tobacco or stone-coloured) suit in a sharp Italian cut which accentuates wide shoulders and narrow hips. Make sure the fabric is impeccable in soft cashmere and silk blends of tweed or attractive cross-weave. Add a really soft white shirt (to highlight the natural tan) which radiates touchability and a silk tie in paisley or other pattern but nothing that has uneasy shapes or colours. Shoes should be plain slip-on with undemonstrative socks. Keep jewellery to a minimum – no bracelets or neck chains and definitely no earrings. Make sure underwear is clean and cotton and don't wear a wimpish vest. Avoid flashy boxer shorts and anything too exotic, such as pastel silk.

Hands should be well manicured – this is essential for any aspiring lover. Hair can follow the prevailing fashion in length but it must be clean and look as if it doesn't need gelling, moussing, spraying or blow-drying. How you smell is important. Nothing too overt. Choose citrus scents or soap mixed with a hint of healthy perspiration from the gym. Nothing rancid. Brush teeth and check breath (too much drink can be as bad as smoking). Details are important, as is behaviour.

Be yourself and make mistakes if necessary. She will find them more endearing than if you try to impress her with over-confidence. Be considerate and leave out details of past conquests or plans for the future, even if they include her. Live in the present, look after her and learn from her. Then leave her without fuss, explanation or recrimination. In other words, with style.

"SO COURT A MISTRESS, SHE DENIES
YOU; LET HER ALONE, SHE WILL COURT YOU."
BEN JOHNSON.

CHAPTER SIX

THAT FINAL
TOUCH
OF STYLE

"Style is charming, well turned out and never
embarrassing. It is something a man should set out to
acquire and does not mean wearing 'sets' of things."

JULIAN CRITCHLEY, MP

The addition of the right accessory is the ultimate stylish complement, so look out for those which are an expression of your own taste and personality.

There are two principal types of dress accessories. The clothing kind – the hats, gloves, scarves etc which complement or complete an outfit – and that extra 'something special', the object which once discovered, becomes a necessity of life. Most such items are small and beautiful and the work of craftsmen. They include items of jewellery and 'useful tools' – a description which covers a multitude of things including cigar cutters and golf umbrellas.

Dress accessories can be used to transform a set of clothes from daytime to evening wear and these include both 'basics' – shoes, belts, ties – and the 'extra' – a bow tie, a jaunty hat – which turn an ordinary outfit into something much more individual, and an expression of your personal style.

CLOTHES ACCESSORIES

HATS. Headgear, once a vital accessory to clothing for the motorist, has come to suffer from the same vehicles that once promoted it. The inconvenience of wearing hats in modern transport has helped in their decline but with their disappearance has also vanished an indication of polite society.

At the end of the nineteenth century, social etiquette for men revolved a good deal around what a man did with his hat, whether he doffed it to acquaintances, removed it in the presence of a lady, or raised it to friends while driving his carriage. Edward VII was apparently adept at removing a cigar from his lips and raising his hat with his whip hand with one sweeping movement while continuing to drive his horses at speed. Not to be tried on the motorway.

Hats lost popularity in this century after the First World War, perhaps because they had been compulsory uniform and men were tired of them. Fitting a hat is an exact science and the trade declined and only survives today at such traditional London establishments as Lock's and Herbert Johnson's. But hats are making a comeback if only for practical reasons. Ten per cent of body heat is lost through the head and hats are practical wear in winter for commuting between heated office and car.

Top hats were much loved by the Victorians who wore them for everything, even gardening. The first policemen wore top hats but they were also adopted by many other groups of working men. They were usually black but some top hats appeared in white and grey and it is the grey version which survives most commonly today as correct wear with a morning coat for formal occasions.

Bowler hats were hated by George V. He called them 'ratcatchers' hats' and refused to allow them into Buckingham Palace. At Lock's, they are traditionally known as 'Cokes' after William Coke who is said to have first commissioned one for his gamekeeper, but it was William Bowler who first manufactured the style. Originally, they were made in grey, brown and black with various kinds of straight or curly brim and were worn in the country as riding hats. Gradually they moved up-market to be worn at race meetings and in the City where they were sometimes called 'business' hats. They were also known as 'billycocks' and in America as a 'Derby'. By the 1930s, the bowler had begun to fall from favour.

Trilby hats replaced the bowler in popularity in the 1930s. Similar to the Homburg but of softer material, the black trilby was made fashionable by Sir Anthony Eden and called an Anthony Eden hat. Edward, Prince of Wales also prefered the trilby and wore it during his tour of Canada in 1919. The Trilby began to make a comeback with Forties- and Fifties-style suits and because of its soft shape is probably still one of the more practical styles. Brown hats have always been traditionally country wear and are still worn at Newmarket.

Straw hats deserve a revival. As men become more aware of the damage of too much sunbathing and seek to protect that tender, balding crown, straw hats can expect to find favour once more. They are romantic items, redolent of sleepy Edwardian summers, flower-filled fourth of Junes and the Eton boating song but their origins are far from glamorous. They began life as butcher's accessories, worn to protect the pate from dripping blood. Panama hats (the best of which are made in the Montechristi district of Ecuador) are the silkier variety of 'straw' which are traditionally made from reed and first became popular in the 1880s. The softer a panama hat, the better it is.

Flat caps have never really recovered from the image of working-class inertia projected by the strip cartoon Andy Capp. The longer-peaked 'shooting' variety is popular with countrymen and in the Sixties caps and Barbours became the uniform of the point-to-point. They were easy to wear in Range Rovers and didn't lose shape when jammed in a pocket. They also had a sort of 'earthy' feel. Yet flat caps *are* unättractive. They make the average man look as if he is wearing a plate on his head and even Captain Mark Phillips cannot give a flat cap style.

Sports hats are perhaps the most popular items of headgear in the modern man's wardrobe. Skiing hats are in a class of their own and range from the practical and ear-preserving to the downright lunatic. Golf caps and hats also come in a wild variety of moods and styles, the most conservative being a version of the flat cap and the most outlandish looking like an Elton John version of a tam-o'-shanter. Football hats and sailing hats are also usually on the wilder side, which is all to the good. The only way to wear this kind of headcovering is with panache (originally meaning 'tuft or plume of feathers, especially as head-dress or on helmet'). Swagger, more than style, is in order and the ability to keep your hat when all about are losing theirs. Funny hats should be encouraged. In a world of uniformity they are a jolly antidote to the serious side of life.

HAIRNOTE: Hairstyles have had much to do with fashions in male headwear. The early eighteenth-century passion for full wigs made hats redundant during the day and nightcaps essential. As hair grew smoother, hats grew higher and by the early nineteenth century when the New York style of wetting the hair and plastering it close to the head was all the rage, hats were important to prevent a man catching his death of cold. In the Sixties and Seventies of the present century, longer hair helped make hats unfashionable (though in the bitter cold winter of 1964, cossack-style fur hats and Tyrolean trilbys had a sudden surge in popularity) but with the return to shorter styles, hats are back on top.

HATS ARE INTERESTING AND ADD
VARIETY TO LIFE.

— FACT AND FANTASY ON HATS —

1 FANTASY: *Wearing a hat makes your hair fall out.*
FACT: Hair loss is genetically determined or sometimes the result of a particular physical condition. Wearing a hat will not make hair fall out though constant friction against a particular patch of hair will not help preserve it.

2 FANTASY: *Wearing a hat makes hair greasy.*
FACT: Greasy hair is usually the result of a scalp condition. It's the scalp which is greasy, not the hair. Washing hair too frequently can aggravate this as some shampoos contain detergents which over-stimulate the scalp. Look for a product that gently conditions the hair. Baby shampoos are not necessarily the answer. They may be too mild to clean hair effectively. Wearing a hat in a hot temperature could cause increased perspiration leading to itching, lank hair. This can be cured by shampooing but the obvious answer is to take the hat off indoors.

3 FANTASY: *Hats make your hair go flat in cold weather.*
FACT: It's static electricity in cold weather which makes hair go flat, though it's true that hats don't help. Most vulnerable is fine, dry hair, which also tends to 'flatten' during air travel. Don't wash hair just before putting on a hat. Using a mousse will help give body.

4 FANTASY: *Hair doesn't need sun protection.*
FACT: Though hair is technically 'dead' it still needs protection from sun and salt, especially if coloured or permed. Wearing a hat also provides protection for the nape of the neck, one of the areas of the body most vulnerable to sunstroke.

High hopes for the short – hats add height. They also attract attention, add wit to an outfit, are used in stylish gestures of courtesy and are the only effective 'antidote' for baldness. Hatters of style: Boy George, Elton John and the late Tommy Trinder.

GLOVES. Like hats, gloves have fallen into disuse with the improvement of transport. Few men now wear gloves for motoring but they do wear them for hunting, playing polo and riding in general. However, the soft glove has slipped from its place in society and hardly gets a mention these days. Woollen gloves and fur-backed mittens have taken over for cold winters but the white cotton gloves, that went so romantically with dress suits in the Thirties, died with Fred Astaire.

This decline of the glove is a great pity as gloves have traditionally had more uses than simple hand coverings. The fashionable 'gauntlet' glove of the sixteenth century for example, was so scalloped and fringed, embroidered and dripping in lace that it might have served equally well as a handkerchief. Gloves have also been used as symbols of aggression (throwing down the gauntlet), deceit (being hand in glove) and nature-loving (foxglove). The most beautiful gloves are made of softest kid, lined with something luxurious like cashmere.

BRACES. Braces come somewhere between being items of clothing and decoration. They were once essential as the only way to hold trousers up but in recent years they have become more ornamental. The revival of Thirties- and Forties-style suits with wider, more voluminous trousers have helped bring braces back into fashion. 'Suspenders' as the Americans call them, along with metal armbands were extremely popular under the double-breasted jacket of the 'gangster' suit but the origin of braces goes back further to revolutionary France.

'Bretelles' were two lengths of ribbon which were fixed on to button holes. They became popular with Napoleon who wore them decorated with the symbol of his native Corsica – the bumble bee. Braces have certain advantages over belts, especially for the more portly figure. They don't cut the silhouette in half and are sometimes more comfortable to wear, but they must be the proper kind – with button-down leather tabs. Metal clip-ons are very cloth-cap-and-pit-boots. 'Twanging' braces is a horrible mannerism, like scratching or picking teeth with a matchstick.

BELTS. Soft and supple leathers in lizard, crocodile and plain black calf with neat, small buckles, are the best belts

BRACES OR 'SUSPENDERS' HAVE COME
BACK INTO FASHION AS A MORE
EFFECTIVE WAY TO HOLD UP TROUSERS
THAN A BELT. BUT AVOID RED ELASTIC
OR METAL CLIPS.

for holding up city trousers. 'Off-duty' belts include the old stretch elastic with the S-bend buckle and canvas belts with leather fastenings. Belt buckles can be a real giveaway. Anything too large and ornate is very Wild West and linking logos are too obvious: the male equivalent of the Louis Vuitton handbag. The webbed army belt is now very Sixties.

SOCKS. *'L'homme peut naître coiffé, mais pas chaussé,* say the French. Socks play an incredibly important role in a man's life considering they are such small and poignant items of clothing.

The history of the sock is long and varied. The Romans wore a kind of sock-sandal called a 'calceus' and persuaded the Ancient Britons to put their feet into untanned, fur-lined leather 'socks' called 'crepeda'. From these, say the French, appeared 'La Chausse', in 1138 precisely. Meanwhile, the 'hose', similar to present-day tights, went from hips to waist and when it became too tight, a gusset was inserted to ease the strain. Enter the codpiece, a small bag with a flap closed by ties. Chaucer's Parson found it all rather excessive and complained about 'the horrible pushed-out testicles that look like the malady of hernia in the wrapping of their hose'. He felt that the effect made the wearer's buttocks resemble 'the hinder parts of a she-ape in the full moon' and also disapproved of the practice of wearing brightly coloured hose with legs of different colours.

Clocked socks, held up with garters or suspenders, became popular in the 1920s. Fortunately, today's socks stand up for themselves. The best materials are still cotton and wool but the addition of nylon in toes and heels is acceptable for 'strength'. Sock length is a matter for debate – to knee, or not to knee? The main criterion is that they should not 'gap' below trousers.

Colours have become much more daring than regulation navy blue and black but brights and pastels need care if worn with city suits. Matching socks to tie is best performed with subtlety. Vivid splashes of red or green are too obvious and the only person who should wear pink socks is the Leander man at Henley Regatta. Better to choose socks that pick up one colour from a patterned tie (preferably not the brightest) so that the 'toning' process goes down gently from the neck to ankle.

SCARVES. Scarves have a definite purpose in life. They bring comfort to the cold collared neck and help prevent throat infections. The warmest scarves are pure cashmere. The most romantic are those wonderful white silk scarves worn with evening dress which translate to studied casualness in daytime. Silk patterned scarves make excellent alternatives to the cravat. They don't leave a 'gap' at the sides of the neck in the way that cravats do and are easy to tie comfortably.

HANDKERCHIEFS. How can anyone be content with blowing their nose on pieces of paper? The woolly bits get caught in the nostrils and when the used wad accidentally goes through the washing machine, it distintegrates into thousands of little white blobs that fasten on to everything else. Ever tried bandaging a child's knee with a piece of paper or offering it to a weeping woman as a consolation prize? Handkerchiefs are *necessary* but not just as ornaments. Nancy Mitford said a gentleman should wear his handkerchief carefully arranged in his top pocket and current fashion has taken this to mean the flaunting of matching sock, tie and kerchief. But this has led to disaster almost as great as the paper variety. Who is going to blow his nose on a square of brightly coloured silk (yellow, covered in red dots that look like a bad nosebleed) or feel at ease using this nouvelle version of the 'buttonhole'? It takes the maxim 'one for blow and one for show' a step too far.

Once gentlemen stopped blowing their noses on their sleeves (Richard II was the first to advise his courtiers that this was unsavoury) handkerchiefs became essential. They also gradually became more frilly, silly, foppy and soppy but they were still *used*. What has now happened to the crisp, clean square of soft white linen, hand-rolled and monogrammed ready to be shaken out when its owner was stirred? The size of a small handtowel and folded in a simple triangle, it peeked reassuringly from a top pocket where it didn't get creased or dirtied by keys and small change. Sadly, it has been replaced by burgundy and paisley silk, by the 'puff' and the 'TV' fold. But Style should never stoop to artifice.

A Touch of Elegance

The man with style carries few accessories but those he has are the very best of their kind. They will have been chosen not only for their beauty but also for their practicality. Most are probably inherited. Some accessories, like the briefcase, go with the job. Others, like studs and cufflinks, are collectors' items.

HANDBAGS. Handbags are the twentieth century's most original contribution to the male wardrobe. Fortunately, they are already fading from the scene. Handbags never really caught on amongst the vast majority of Englishmen but there was an unnerving moment when natty little leather handbags with wrist straps were *the* stylish accessory for the international jetset. At least, this kind was preferable to the

BLENDING NEUTRAL COLOURS AND
TEXTURES LOOKS ELEGANT BUT THE
OCCASIONAL CONTRACT CAN ALSO ADD
A TOUCH OF STYLE.

strapped shoulder bags which came 'swinging' into the Sixties. However, there was a false premise behind the entire handbag-for-men concept.

The idea was that a man could empty his pockets and thus prevent unsightly bulges in his trousers. However, this only applied to those wearing tight garments which were essentially un-English. For the man dressed more traditionally in trousers that gave room to put hands in pockets, the handbag was unnecessary and, more to the point, unmanly. As a British Ambassador once observed on seeing a colleague carrying a wrist-strap bag: 'Good God. Wet enough to shoot snipe off.'

BRIEFCASES. Briefcases, on the other hand, are perfectly acceptable and almost as indicative of character and social status as the old school tie. The most traditional kind are those of squashy leather which have straps and locks and look like music cases. They are official issue to diplomats and only ever have two sets of keys. The diplomatic 'bag' has an attractive OHMS badge on the front and a pocket in which the present incumbent can place his namecard. Inside, he keeps his credentials – newspaper, sandwiches and a copy of the latest spy scandal.

International man carries a piece of understated style in finest calf with gunmetal locks and rare craftsmanship revealed in the close stitching on the leather. His briefcase is never scuffed or battered. It contains a set of small luxury items in matching calf – billfold, wallet, address book and key case and is notable for its lack of 'fuss'. Quiet and distinguished, it exudes a combination of secure confidence.

The aspiring financial genius carries the latest Hi-Tech style: rounded front corners, matt black quick-set combination locks, black metal corner protectors and a

REAL LUGGAGE FOR REAL TRAVELLERS
COMES IN SERIOUS SIZES AND IS NEVER
CARRIED BY ITS OWNER.

moulded handle. Inside (lined in soft pigskin) there are pen pockets, space for a Time Manager and a false bottom.

The best briefcases are leather and the modern box shape is more secure than the old hard-framed lid-over-body design which was a descendant of the Gladstone bag. Plastic briefcases and carrier bags (even designer ones) lack style.

LUGGAGE. The best luggage is neat, compact and versatile. Gone are the days when tin trunks and battered leather suitcases followed their owners about the world. The 'status symbol' luggage – that which is instantly identified by a thousand logos – is also on its way out. Style lies in individuality and not in over-zealous name-branding. Everyone knows that travellers always return from their journey with more luggage, so bags which fold into other bags are an essential part of the experienced traveller's equipment.

Canvas is hardwearing and lighter to carry than a hard-sided suitcase, but air travel has made one particular item of luggage absolutely essential. This is the luxury 'cabin' bag, a once-in-a-lifetime indulgence that accompanies one through life like a constant friend. It can be in suede-lined specially grained leather; in silk-lined calf; soft, squashy and shoulder-strapped in mock lambskin, lizard or crocodile or – the ultimate – a traditional Gladstone shape in softest skin. If current price is prohibitive, search for secondhand or beg, borrow or steal from elderly relatives. Carry it everywhere. Modern transport systems (apart from the private jet) don't do much for 'heirloom luggage' so keep to canvas for the hold but indulge in just one, small, piece of perfection for carrying by hand. It will do wonders for the right impression when casually placed by the hotel reception desk. After all, what Head Porter is going to pop outside to check which BMW is yours?

JEWELLERY. Tricky subject. There is, of course, the Cartier Set. Gold this and that, panthers on stick pins, all a bit over the top and vaguely 'new'. Then there's the City signet ring – not-so-old gold. A favourite amongst the pushier junk bond dealers, it makes them feel established – something to hock after the crash. The danger lies in looking like a 'Macaroni', the eighteenth-century version of the confidence trickster. The solution is to keep jewellery discreet, old and preferably of a military design (medals are still the best decoration).

THE WATCH

The one piece of jewellery that is definitely acceptable. Well, almost. The Rolex crowd have taken things a bit too far, leaving men limp-wristed with the weight. Heavy metal also got into sports with watches that had the elegance of a set of shock absorbers. At the other extreme came the Black Plastics, minimalism that somehow lost its value when overprinted to order with personalised messages like 'I love you' and 'Bog off matey'. But happily for sanity, there remain watches that quietly combine the best of British design with Swiss precision and are made of recognisably good materials such as Sheffield steel and gold.

The quartz watch demolished concern with accuracy and did away with many a pleasant pastime associated with watches – peering at them intently, shaking them and holding them up to the ear. A pocket watch was once a sign of prosperity and watch chains gave an air of civic responsibility. Victorian Hunters are now collectors' pieces but any good watch should last a lifetime.

Look for style that won't date too quickly – plain-faced with Roman numerals, elegant enough to wear with a dress shirt but equally compatible with sports clothes. Avoid the 'watch wardrobe' concept. It indicates indecision.

A word on bracelets. Those heavy chain identity bracelets that first clanked their way into view in the Sixties have never been items of style. The only men who wear bracelets are those detained at Her Majesty's pleasure. Stylish men just don't wear bracelets, pendants, earrings, safety pins or trinkets of a religious nature.

STUDS AND RINGS

Most antique cufflinks around today originated in the nineteenth century when gold was fashionable. Cufflinks of this period were either plain and engraved or set with semi-precious stones such as citrines and yellow beryls. Bold designs emerged in the Edwardian period in exotic enamels, and with Art Deco came a preference for platinum and diamonds.

Signet rings were used for identification long before writing became the rage. Originally they bore a red seal or crest. Wartski of London's Bond Street still sell eighteenth- and nineteenth-century signet rings and 'intaglios' (meaning engraved). Tessier's stock modern signet rings and Asprey's have created their own contemporary range set with coloured stones like cornelians. Lapis lazuli is also popular. The Prince of Wales wears a fine signet ring which he constantly 'turns' in moments of anxiety. Other men fiddle with their cufflinks. This is expensive body language.

STICK PINS AND TIE CLIPS

Stick pins are beautiful. Many have sporting motifs, foxes, hunting scenes, diamond studded game birds, wild duck crystals and golden birds of prey. Others reflect the particular 'crazes' of the Victorian and Edwardian eras and show penny-farthing bicycles or golf clubs.

Stick pins were originally used to secure cravats. Nowadays, they also make interesting lapel wear and can be used on a plain tie. Most are about two inches long with a 'twist' in the middle to help hold the pin in the cloth. Modern tie pins are shaped like brooches and have a small chain to help anchor the tie.

Tie clips that clamp on to the side of the tie had a revival with the Teddy Boys whose long jackets almost mimicked the frock coats of the Edwardian age. Tie clips are not worn much today. If cravats make the comeback they deserve, stick pins could return to high fashion.

THE BRIGHTER BROLLY. CHEERFUL,
PRACTICAL AND USER-FRIENDLY.

STICKS AND UMBRELLAS. The umbrella has come to be a symbol of masculinity in the City but originally it had to struggle for recognition in a man's wardrobe. Parasols date back to antiquity but they were essentially feminine accessories. Folding umbrellas made of oilcloth first appeared in the 1760s but they were scorned. Men preferred to carry sticks or canes and thought the umbrella was effete. Furled black umbrellas with knotted cane or leather handles became the uniform of the City gentleman. Then in the Sixties, this mark of style was replaced by flat or round collapsible types which could disappear into a briefcase. Many of them opened on a dangerous spring which shot the canopy out like a parachute. Fortunately, golf umbrellas also became popular. Brightly coloured, straight handled, vast, they are cheerful, practical and can easily accommodate two people.

The walking stick is another item of elegance which has largely disappeared. Sticks today are strictly for country walking, an alternative to a gun or a scythe, used for swiping at the undergrowth or throwing for the dog to fetch.

SPECTACLES. Designer fever hit spectacles in the Eighties, aided by legislation which ended the opticians' monopoly and helped change the way we look. Glasses became *the* accessory. The rich and famous hid behind them, the not-so-rich and famous wore them in hope that they might be mistaken for someone rich and famous. A good pair of sunglasses with light, flexible frame and brown glass (still the best colour to protect eyes) was less important than the letters stamped on the side. These ranged from CD *(Corps Diplomatique)* to YSL (Young Socialist League), though Bruce Oldfield, who also has a range of designer frames, wisely avoided the initial game. But make and model are less important than shape and comfort, especially for glasses.

Over twelve million men wear spectacles in the UK – some people just cannot get along with contact lenses but a much larger proportion of the public wear sunglasses and these should also be chosen with care.

Look for a solid saddle bridge which helps prevent glasses slipping down the nose, for an eye-shape that is suitable for prescription lenses, for glasses made in a material that won't break when accidentally sat upon or crushed in a pocket. Glasses can improve looks as well as sight. Talk of 'face shapes' is largely uninstructive but common sense dictates a few obvious 'rules'.

Emphasis on the vertical lines of the frame helps 'stretch' round faces, square shapes emphasise a square jaw. Strong horizontal lines help balance a long face. Small features benefit from a rimless style of spectacle. Long noses are 'shortened' by a low saddle bridge (in the middle of the glasses, rather than running along the top of the frame) while a 'keyhole' bridge will give an impression of length. Finally, think about hair colour. If, for example, hair is very dark, sombre frames will emphasise a heavy impression. The best way to choose spectacle frames is by trying them on and deciding which look best and which feel most comfortable. Give thought to when the glasses will be worn. It may be necessary to have different frames for work and sport.

The most popular shape for glasses in Britain, according to manufacturers, is the classic wide-eyed and deep

Men can look very appealing in
the right specs but choose a pair
that fit properly and sit
comfortably across the bridge of
the nose.

look. Slightly geometric, with an anatomical bridge and bespoke contouring, they look serious and sincere.

Though men may not make passes at girls who wear glasses, women it seems, are attracted to the bespectacled male. Psychologists think it hints at vulnerability, intellectualism and even gentleness, all qualities, curiously enough, portrayed by Tony Curtis masquerading as a millionaire in 'Some Like It Hot'. Only Marilyn Monroe could have turned his glasses into barometers of desire.

PIPES AND CIGARETTE HOLDERS. 'He looked out at the beautiful day and consumed half a pint of iced orange juice, three scrambled eggs and bacon and a double portion of coffee without sugar. He lit his first cigarette, a Balkan and Turkish mixture, specially made for him . . .'

Everything that James Bond does in the above paragraph is wrong by the dictates of today. First of all, he is relaxing when he should already be at a busy desk. Second, the breakfast: 'iced' orange juice, too cold for the stomach and probably killing the vitamin C content; eggs and bacon, high

THE ALL-PURPOSE PIPE. EVEN IF YOU
DON'T SMOKE, YOU CAN USE IT AS A
DIETARY AID (SOMETHING TO CHEW ON
BETWEEN MEALS) AND A WEAPON
AGAINST STRESS.

in cholesterol, a heart attack on a plate; coffee, a kick-start cuppa high in caffeine; a 'double portion', oh dear. As for the cigarette, a cancer stick – a real Doctor No No.

The modern version of James Bond, as portrayed in the film series, is far removed from the character created by Ian Fleming which largely reflected Fleming's own lifestyle. Cecil Beaton's portrait of Fleming shows a sophisticated man in evening dress, smoking a cigarette through a holder, a study in elegant languor. Today's Bond leaps through life in a whirlwind of fast cars, women and wild gadgetry at a pace that is almost as lethal as smoking.

Smoking was once an art. Tobacco mixtures were as varied and individual as wines. Lighters were ingenious devices, the best incorporating a horizontal flint wheel which allowed the user to hold and ignite with one hand. Cigarette holders were standard to help cut nicotine and keep a gentleman's hand free from stains, and cigarettes were kept in smart, spring-locking cases instead of battered cartons. Quality was important, not excess. A good cigarette was enjoyed and appreciated like a fine glass of wine and as remote from the concept of the 'duty-free two hundred' as claret from Bulgarian red.

Pipe smoking has always been a masculine pursuit. Women who smoke pipes are either highly pretentious, or like the ladies of Queen Elizabeth I's court and George Eliot, strong, dominant characters.

Briar pipes are made from the hard, dry, mature roots of *Erica arboria*, the best of which are over a hundred years old and which look like giant truffles. A long process of boiling and selecting the wood plus a great deal of craftsmanship goes into the making of each pipe. Alfred Dunhill spent three years evolving the complicated skills which characterise his company's pipe-making. He experimented with endless mouth-pieces and these are still individually matched to each bowl and marked with their characteristic 'white spot' which indicates the top.

The paraphernalia of pipe smoking takes it into the realms of science. There are soft black nappa tobacco pouches, pewter pipe rests and knock-out ash bowls, tobacco jars, pipe-care cloths impregnated with a special wax for buffing, high-density chenille cotton pipe cleaners, pipe knifes and carbon cutters, pipe tampers and dottlers for cleaning, pipe inner tubes, pipe mouthpiece polish, spills and long safety matches for lighting and even packets of hand wipes. Everything, in fact, to make a pipe smoker pause for serious thought between puffs.

CIGARS. It was Kipling who immortalised cigars with the words 'a woman is only a woman but a good cigar is a smoke', and whose stories of the East may have given rise to the myth that Burma cheroots are rolled on a dusky female thigh. In fact, they are rather more prosaically rolled with moisture pads on boards.

Veteran smokers tend to go for the large nine-inch cigars with exotic names like the Belicoso or the Fabuloso. The beginner is best advised to start with a smaller, lighter Havana, like the Rafael Gonzalez and to take note of the following tips:

1 Buy a cigar cutter. The end of the cigar should be clipped to allow it to draw. A clean round cut is best. The V-cut sharpens the flavour of the cigar too much and is, as the experts say, like drinking claret through a staw.

2 Char the end of the cigar, then allow it to draw while rotating it. Never inhale. The enjoyment of a good cigar comes from its flavour and aroma. The fact that cigar smoke should never touch the lungs is why many insurance companies make exceptions for cigar smokers.

3 Only smoke the first two-thirds. Allow the end to burn out.

4 Store cigars in a humidor, or away from direct heat and light at least. The top of a dark cupboard may do but looking after cigars is much more complicated than laying down wine as every cigar has a different maturing age. A Bolivar, for example, will continue to mature after fifteen years, whereas the Rafael mentioned above will start 'dying' after six years. Only experience will help to appreciate the difference in taste.

Last word on smoking. 'When' to smoke is now largely a matter of personal preference and politeness to others, but there are still some occasions when the unofficial 'no-smoking' rule should continue to apply – in church, in hospital and at a formal banquet before a toast to the Queen. If it seems odd and old-fashioned to mention them here, the excuse is that even in this thrusting age, there is still room for a few good manners, such as *not* stubbing out cigarettes in other people's plants, saucers or dinner plates, *not* blowing smoke directly into the eyes of the nearest person, *not* sticking cigarette ends behind the ear, and having 'smoky' clothes regularly cleaned. Some might even go further and add the desire to see smoking practised in private and only between consenting adults.

DESK ACCESSORIES. The items on a man's desk are as indicative of character as the contents of a woman's handbag. The Super-successful Man of Style sits behind a Power Desk. Black, clean lines, vast and programmed with technology like the flight deck of Concorde. Matching leather blotter, letter tray, tub of well-sharpened pencils and a special holder for namecards. In the centre of the desk the one essential item of personal style – the gold fountain pen. 'Plastics' are for the plebs.

Since Big Bang and the Stock Market Crash, everyone is familiar with the City desk. Cramped cubby-holes littered with VDUs in acres of space to allow the telly cameras room to film the action. In October '87, this was the rat race at work. Young men in shirt sleeves rushed about with paper in their mouths while an 'expert' stood in front of the camera adjusting his tie for the evening news. The city slicker sat at a rentadesk and when the stock market wasn't crashing, life was a jolly round of strippergrams, super orders of Big Macs, temperamental outbursts and Hamlet cigars. Now it's all more serious and the yuppies are gone with their toys – telephones that speak to you across a crowded room and oscillating balls that go ping.

FRAGRANCE

Success today smells much sweeter. British men who were once hard-pressed to use a deodorant are now more 'body aware' and recognise that fragrance is an important part of 'image' and the ultimate in accessories.

Sales of 'male fragrance' rose significantly in the Eighties to make up 35 per cent of an equally burgeoning market in 'male toiletries'. The cause was two-fold.

First, the 'sports boom' made men more aware of their personal level of health and fitness and less inclined to associate scent with cissiness. Men began to explore and experiment, though aftershave remained the bestseller in Britain with cologne the worldwide favourite. Even so, there were still those reluctant to indulge in too much 'personal freshness'. Dunhill, whose Edition brand outstripped all its French competitors in the first half of 1987, discovered that 86 per cent of British golfers used an aftershave but only 60 per cent of them were prepared to take a shower after making the eighteenth hole. 'Sporting' fragrances included Polo, Guerlain's Derby, Björn Borg's 6–0 and Lacoste.

Secondly, men began at last to buy for themselves. Led by the nose for too long, they responded to marketing which displayed men's toiletries alongside clothes, thereby highlighting their role as important accessories. Once he became interested, the Englishman went straight to the top. Fifty-six per cent of the fragrance purchases made by men for themselves in 1987 were 'up-market' names. Good grooming, which included smelling well, was a sign of success, and the business man not only wore the designer pinstripe, he purchased the 'career fragrance' to match.

Fashion and fragrance are natural companions. Both express the user's personality and convey positive messages through non-verbal language. Coco Chanel is often credited with launching the first 'designer' fragrance but it was in fact a man, the incomparable Paul Poiret, who introduced the first designer perfume back in 1911. He emphasised 'good taste' and his own good taste convinced him that fragrance was 'the necessary complement to elegance'.

Fragrance for men relies a good deal on the power of the label. The name conjures up a whole range of image-building concepts, including masculinity (Macho, Brut), manly odours (Old Spice, Wild Moss, English Leather), godliness, always next to cleanliness, (Kouros, Antaeus) and increasingly, straightforward names that the buyer can immediately identify with a particular image in clothes and lifestyle – Armani, Versace, Givenchy and Chanel Gentleman.

This is partly because a man wants everything he buys or wears to say something about him, but it also stems

FRAGRANCE IS OFTEN ASSOCIATED
WITH THE MAN OF POETIC SOUL, THE
NATURE-LOVER WHO IS MORE AT HOME
IN A FIELD OF DAISIES THAN THE SHOP
FLOOR OF THE MANUFACTURING PLANT.
BUT PERSONAL FRESHNESS IS FOR
EVERYONE AND BEING CLEAN IS A
PREREQUISITE OF STYLE – HOWEVER
YOU DRESS.

from the Englishman's uncertainty about the effect that wearing fragrance might have on his masculinity.

Gradually, however, the obsession with 'manliness' and with smelling only of 'free labours and manly exercise' as Socrates put it, has given way to an appreciation of subtler scents. Many of the ingredients of current favourites in men's aftershaves and *eaux de toilettes* are the same 'feminine' notes that appear in women's perfumes – carnation, bergamot, amber, lavender and geranium. It is the way they are blended that makes the difference. Every perfume has a top, bottom and middle note. The first gives the initial impression, the second indicates whether the fragrance is predominantly 'masculine' or 'feminine' and the third is the 'dried-out note' which eventually gives the fragrance its character.

Young men, in particular, are much more self-assured about fragrance than their fathers. Fragrance for men fell from favour during the two world wars and has taken a long time to recover. Before that, Victorian men used fragrance indirectly – on clothes and in hair oils and the Regency man either loved or loathed perfume. Beau Brummell found it 'unnatural' for a man to use fragrance but many of his contemporaries were addicted to Hungary water, rose-water and eau-de-Cologne which was also used as a cure for a hangover and as a mouthwash.

The perfume company Haarmann and Reimer whose four-volume work is the contemporary authority on the subject, identified four types of modern fragrance-users. First, the soap and water brigade for whom cleanliness is a function like eating and drinking and who do not perfume themselves at all. Second, those who use fragrance only for specific occasions. Third, the brand-name users who use fragrance to project a particular image, and finally the 'perfume aesthetes' who use fragrance to satisfy a special mood or feeling.

In a dramatically short space of time, the 'style-conscious' moved swiftly from first 'carbolic' base to somewhere between third and last. While not yet 'perfume aesthetes', perhaps, most men of today are certainly brand users and very definite about which brand they like. Whereas the Sixties were awash with overpowering aftershaves that were barely preferable to BO, Eighties man has shown a definite preference for the British 'classic'.

Jermyn Street once again became a male 'fashion' centre, this time as much for fragrance as for clothes. 'Traditional' fragrances from Floris, Czech and Speake, and Dunhill with notes of citrus and sandalwood began to compete subtly with the overtones of musk and chypre. The Englishman began to follow his own nose and it led him straight back to the 'classics'.

Psychologists have had a field day with the 'power' of perfume and the way that scent can attract or repel.

Pheromones, the scent signals used by some creatures to attract each other, became the subject of eager discussion. Boar sprays were developed to encourage pigs to mate and an American company tried to adapt the principle to perfume. Unfortunately, what worked for wildlife seemed to have less effect on the human bore and scent selection remained a highly subjective process.

Appreciation of smell seems largely based on association. The attempt to encapsulate perfection through scent can become obsessive as writers from Proust to Patrick Süskind have shown. But manufacturers have been quick to realise that for a luxury item like scent, bottle design, packaging and colour of presentation are almost as important as the contents themselves.

Men's fragrance, like women's, divides into a range of scent 'families'. These vary from the sharp, fresh 'green' to the heavier 'musk' notes. Each family has had its favourites. Eau Sauvage, worn by men and loved by women, belongs to the cool, floral citrus family. Old Spice belongs to the Oriental-sweet family. Aramis and Polo belong to the chypre family, a sophisticated mixture of leather and fresh pine, and Paco Rabanne and Brut are part of the fern or 'fougère' family.

Men who are attracted to a particular female fragrance could look amongst these families for the masculine version as many fragrances for men are descendants of perfumes for women. Old Spice, for example, comes from the same family as one of the greatest female classics, Guerlain's Shalimar. Aramis is a direct descendant of Cabochard by the designer Madame Grès and Dunhill's first fragrance for men, launched in 1934, belongs to the same family as Chanel No. 5.

PURCHASING POWER. The best way to buy aftershave and *eau de toilette* is to experiment. Take advantage of 'sampling' in stores and avoid embarrassment by heading for the specialist men's shops or menswear departments. Don't be overawed by packaging. It's the contents that count, not the bottle. Few men give thought to how to use fragrance. After shaving is obvious, but this need not be confined to morning practice. Some men like to shave in the evening before going out when a warmer, muskier fragrance might be more appropriate. Women have come to appreciate the lifestyle concept of perfumes, building a 'wardrobe' of scents for different uses. Why shouldn't men do the same with aftershaves?

Fresh, citrussy scents not only make the wearer feel more 'alive' at eight-thirty in the morning, they are infinitely preferable to stand next to on public transport than the heavier, sweeter variety. No man wants to stride into the boardroom smelling potently of something that comes on stronger than he does, but a crisp, clean fragrance can add to a business-like impression.

Off duty, the more old-fashioned notes are subtly effective. Rose-water is one of the oldest scents. Delicate and rich, it breathes good grooming and can often be detected in the cashmere corners of smart New York department stores. Flowers of one sort or another appear in most fragrances so it is no more 'unmanly' to wear them occasionally as single notes and the effect can be startling.

HOW TO USE

1 Don't pour half a pint into the hands and slap it on. It's a waste and the effect can be overpowering. Dab it on a little at a time, using fingertips or cotton wool.

2 Keep the top on the bottle after use. All fragrance evaporates and though the actual fragrance content of aftershave and eau de toilette is very low, it will disappear just as rapidly. For this reason it's also better to keep it in the bathroom cabinet (but not above the radiator or near a light) than on the bathroom shelf.

3 Try to match deodorant, aftershave, soap, talc etc. One smell, carefully 'layered' is preferable to a conflicting collection.

4 Repeat of number one. The man with style prefers moderation in most things. Aftershaves fade quickly but that first impression can be an alcoholic assault to the nostrils. The best fragrances 'die down' to a longer-lasting, subtle scent that is particularly pleasant in proximity.

THE ENGLISHMAN RELAXED IN HIS OWN
STYLE – YOU'VE COME A LONG WAY
BROTHER!

SELECTED BIBLIOGRAPHY

HISTORY OF MEN'S COSTUME, *Marion Sichel*. Batsford 1984

EVERYDAY DRESS 1650-1900, *Elizabeth Ewing*, Batsford 1984

ARMY UNIFORMS OF WORLD WAR II, *Andrew Mollo and Malcom McGregor*, Blandford Press 1973

ARMY UNIFORMS OF WORLD WAR I, *Andrew Mollo and Pierre Turner*, Blandford Press 1977

FASHION FOR MEN, AN ILLUSTRATED HISTORY, *Diane de Marly*, Batsford Press 1985

THE ENGLISH GENTLEMAN, *Douglas Sutherland*, Debrett 1978

DEBRETT'S CORRECT FORM, Futura Publications Limited 1970

THE BEST MAN'S DUTIES, *Vernon Heaton*, Elliot Right Way Books

STYLE WARS, *Peter York*, Sidgwick and Johnson Ltd, 1980

THE OFFICIAL SLOANE RANGER HANDBOOK, *Ann Barr and Peter York*, Ebury Press, 1982

CLASS, *Jilly Cooper*, Eyre Methuen Ltd 1979

THE ENGLISH SEASON, *Godfrey Smith*, Pavilion Books Ltd 1987

THE BOOK OF TIES, *Davide Mosconi and Riccardo Villarosa*, Tie Rack Ltd, 1985

THE OLD SCHOOL, *Simon Raven*, Hamish Hamilton, 1986

COLOUR FOR MEN, *Carole Jackson with Kalia Lulow*, Colour Me Beautiful Inc, 1984

OUR FAMILY BUSINESS, *Mary Dunhill*, The Bodley head, 1979

THE GENTLE ART OF SMOKING, *Alfred H. Dunhill*, The Bodley head

FULLY FIT IN 60 MINUTES, The Complete Shape-Up programme for Men, *Todd Estabrook*, Thorson's Publishing Group, 1984

THE HAIR CARE SYSTEM, *Larry Geller*, Holistic Health Systems 1981

THE BOOK OF THE COURTIER, *Castiglione*, (translated by Charles S Singelton) Anchor Books, 1959

NOBLESSE OBLIGE, *Nancy Mitford*, Hamish Hamilton, 1956

MANNERS FOR MEN, *Mrs Humphrey*, (1897) reprinted by Webb and Bower, 1979

ETIQUETTE HANDBOOK, *Barbara Cartland*, Paul Hamlyn, 1962

CASINO ROYALE, *Ian Fleming*, Pan Books Limited 1955

THUNDERBALL, *Ian Fleming*, Pan Books Limited 1968

DIAMONDS ARE FOREVER, *Ian Fleming*, Triad/Panther Books 1977

A GENTLEMAN'S WARDROBE, *Paul Keers*, Weidenfeld and Nicholson 1987